Praise for *Fly!*

"I love a book written by a smart woman who reinvented herself. Steph Wagner's debut book, *Fly!* is not only a cautionary tale about every woman's need to claim her financial independence, it's also a triumphant story about one women's journey to self-confidence and her mission to share the hard lessons she's learned with women everywhere. That's true girl power."
—Bobbi Brown, Makeup Artist and Founder, Jones Road Beauty

"*Fly!* is both an essential, everywoman's guide to financial literacy and a moving memoir about how one woman rebuilt her life after things fell apart. With candor and courage, Steph Wagner shares her story of persisting through the hard times, as she offers practical, grounded advice about achieving financial autonomy. It's an inspiring and useful book for women of all generations."
—Cheryl Strayed, #1 *New York Times* Bestselling Author, *Wild*

"Steph's story proves that it's never too late to rise, rebuild, and reclaim your power. *Fly!* is a powerful guide for creating a life you love—on your own terms."
—Candace Nelson, Founder, Sprinkles and Pizzana, and Bestselling Author, *Sweet Success*

"As a stay-at-home mom with three young children, Steph Wagner saw her enviable life suddenly destroyed when her husband left her for another woman and abandoned his financial responsibilities to the family that depended on him. The story of how Wagner took charge of their economic survival and created an even better new life from the wreckage is a powerful inspiration for anyone who's dealt with unexpected loss—but it's also an invaluable how-to guide for everyone on building financial stability and the freedom to live your most cherished dreams. As kind and reassuring as your most sympathetic friend, Wagner takes her readers by the hand and walks them safely through the minefield of money and its mysteries. She's the ultimate role model, because she's been there, but she also has a rare gift for explaining complex issues in clear, understandable language as she simplifies and demystifies the financial challenges that make so many of us want to start screaming or hide our heads in the sand. *Fly!* is the perfect guide to help you deal with disaster and turn adversity into good fortune—and it's a must-read for anyone who's ready to build the life of her dreams."
—Leslie Bennetts, Award-Winning Journalist and Bestselling Author, *The Feminine Mistake* and *Last Girl Before Freeway*

"*Fly!* is not just a book—it's a lifeline and a guide. Steph Wagner brings together financial expertise and hard-earned life experience to speak to women at every intersection—whether you're running a business, a household, starting over, or simply reimagining what's next. This is not just a book about women in business—it's for women in life. With clarity, empathy, and practicality, Steph meets you where you are and shows you how to move forward with intention."

—Chanel Frazier, Founder, CHF Ventures and
former Managing Director, BlackRock

"I laughed, I cried—and, most importantly, I learned more about setting myself up for financial independence and long-term success than I did in twelve years of private school. Steph's story is powerful. She shares openly and vulnerably, offering valuable tools and insights that give women the chance to learn critical financial lessons we're somehow expected to just 'know.' From me—and all the women who don't consider themselves financially savvy—thank you, Steph, for writing this book."

—Lucy Burke, Southern Methodist University, Class of 2023

"From beginning to end, *Fly!* feels like a conversation with your best friend combined with that Finance 101 course—which, four years after college, I've completely forgotten. It's raw, real, and deeply human—the story of someone who's been there, lived it, survived it, and then some. But it's not a story shared for sympathy; it's shared in solidarity. Steph took the pain from the worst moments of her life and turned it into purpose—and ultimately, joy for herself and a road map for the rest of us. *Fly!* is a love letter to all women, empowering each of us to build a life of abundance. And all we have to do is start."

—Abbey McKean, Texas Christian University, Class of 2021

"Steph's story captured me and pulled me in within the first few pages. I found myself craving more after each chapter. I actually forgot I was reading a book about financial literacy, financial independence, and financial security—it felt like I was hearing a close friend share her life story. Her words and life experiences are powerful and deeply relatable. I learned so much from her financial expertise, yet I never felt like I should already know this stuff. Instead, I felt like I had a friend I could ask anything—someone who truly understands where I'm coming from. I have a 25-year-old daughter, and I can't wait for her to read it. No one should wait until they're older, widowed, or divorced to become financially literate. Steph's book is approachable, engaging, and essential—for all women and young adults."

—Kelly Topfer, Wife, Mother, and Volunteer

Fly!

Fly!

A Woman's Guide to
Financial Freedom and
Building a Life You Love

STEPH WAGNER

MATT HOLT

Matt Holt Books
An Imprint of BenBella Books, Inc.
Dallas, TX

Fly! copyright © 2025 by Stephanie Lynn Wagner

MATT HOLT BENBELLA

Matt Holt is an imprint of BenBella Books, Inc.
8080 N. Central Expressway
Suite 1700
Dallas, TX 75206
benbellabooks.com
Send feedback to feedback@benbellabooks.com

BenBella and *Matt Holt* are federally registered trademarks.

Printed in the United States of America
10 9 8 7 6 5 4 3 2 1

Library of Congress Control Number: 2025020854
ISBN 9781637747650 (hardcover)
ISBN 9781637747667 (electronic)

Editing by Katie Dickman
Copyediting by Jessica Easto
Proofreading by Ashley Casteel and Marissa Wold Urhina
Text design and composition by PerfecType, Nashville, TN
Cover design by Morgan Carr
Printed by Lake Book Manufacturing

Special discounts for bulk sales are available. Please contact bulkorders@benbellabooks.com.

To Dillon, Cole, and Drew,
May you always think big, chase your dreams fearlessly, and
never stop believing in yourselves. Because if you can dream it,
you can achieve it. My love for you is limitless—you are the
reason I found the strength to rise when it felt impossible.
Thank you for being my heart's greatest inspiration.

And to all the women who've walked a similar path
and those still finding their way—this is for you.
Live boldly. FLY!

Contents

Vision without action is merely a dream.
Action without vision just passes the time.
Vision with action can change the world.

———————————

—Joel Barker, author and futurist, *The Power of Vision*

Foreword

When I was a little girl, I didn't dream of boardrooms or balance sheets. I dreamed in color—sparkly dresses, bright lipstick, and the magic of self-expression through fashion. I was a playful kid who thrived on creativity, whether it was color-coding my closet or sketching new ideas in the margins of my notebooks. But if you had asked me then where I saw myself as an adult, there is no way that becoming the founder of a global jewelry brand or navigating the financial intricacies that come with scaling a multimillion-dollar business would have been on my vision board. Honestly, I wouldn't have even known what those words meant.

So I didn't set out to be a founder or CEO—I set out to create beautiful things. First it was hats. And I realized that we no longer lived in the 1940s, and most people didn't wear hats. My business tanked within five years. But I quickly learned that failure is a bridge: If I hadn't had that experience, I wouldn't be where I am today. Like so many women who find themselves at the helm of something bigger than they ever planned, I learned quickly that passion alone wouldn't pay the bills or fund the future I dreamed of.

When I began designing jewelry pieces from my spare bedroom, I poured every ounce of my creative energy into unique gemstone shapes and color palettes. I was completely immersed in the artistry, and pretty much unaware of what it would take financially to turn this dream into something sustainable. The turning point came when I realized I needed a line of credit just to keep going. And when I walked into that bank, I wasn't just asking for money—I was asking for belief. As a new business owner with no formal education in finance, the whole process felt over-whelming. I had to put everything I owned on the line as collateral. It was terrifying. But it was also the moment I realized that understanding money—how it works, how to talk about it, how to make it work for *you*—wasn't optional. It was essential.

And it's in that space—where creativity meets financial literacy—that I've come to believe some of the most powerful growth happens. That's also where Steph Wagner comes in.

I met Steph several years ago, and our friendship has grown through our shared work to support women's economic empowerment. She has become a frequent speaker at the University of Texas's Kendra Scott Women's Entrepreneurial Leadership Institute, and I've partnered with her on impactful Northern Trust events dedicated to helping female founders. From the start, I knew she wasn't your typical financial expert. She didn't just talk numbers—she talked *life*. She connected with our students not just through education but through empathy. Over time, we connected on a deeper level too, realizing that we both experienced personal heartache that could have destroyed us. We both became single mothers early in our careers. Each of us raised three boys, and we have both had this experience during very hard times: looking into the little faces of our kids and realizing failure was *not* an option.

That kind of experience changes you. It becomes your "why." It lights a fire in you to succeed not in spite of the challenges but *because* of them.

What I love most about Steph—and what you'll feel in every page of this book—is that she doesn't separate finance from real life. She knows that talking about money isn't just about interest rates and investment strategies (although yes, those matter). It's about independence. It's about security. It's about being able to make choices for yourself—whether that's starting a business, leaving a toxic relationship, or sending your kids to college.

This book isn't just a guide. It's a road map. It's full of tangible steps, real-life stories, and the kind of practical wisdom that makes you feel like you're having coffee with a really smart, really honest friend. Steph doesn't shy away from the hard stuff, either. She knows the barriers women face. From the staggering statistic that only 2 percent of venture capital goes to women, to the way many of us were raised not to talk about money at all, there are very real reasons why so many women feel behind financially. And yet, she offers a way forward that feels empowering, not shaming.

That message resonates deeply with me. When I was building my company, I often felt like I was making it up as I went along. And in a way, I was. I leaned on mentors, asked a thousand questions, and made a ton of mistakes. But I also had an incredible tribe of people around me—my parents, my best friends, and especially my kids—who believed in me even when I was still learning to believe in myself. I talk about this often when I speak publicly: Entrepreneurship can feel like a solo journey, but it never is. My success is just as much theirs as it is mine.

That's why, as my company grew, I was intentional about building a culture that reflects those same values. Today, over 90 percent of my team are women. That didn't happen by accident. It happened because I remembered what it was like to be a working mom with limited support. I wanted to build a place where family, fashion, and philanthropy could all coexist—where women could bring their full selves to work and be celebrated for it.

And that's exactly what Steph is doing through this book. She's creating a space where women can show up as they are—whether they're just starting out or rebuilding after a major life change—and be met with tools, guidance, and encouragement to take ownership of their financial future.

The truth is, even with all the success I've been fortunate to experience, I still get nervous about money sometimes. I still feel the weight of responsibility that comes with leading a company and making decisions that affect so many people. But I've learned that being nervous isn't a weakness—it's a sign that you care. It means you're invested. It means you're human.

And that's why I believe this book is essential right now. Because in a world where uncertainty can feel like the only constant—where the stock market fluctuates wildly and the financial headlines are often overwhelming—we need voices like Steph's to bring clarity, compassion, and confidence back into the conversation.

So to every woman holding this book, let me just say: You don't need to have it all figured out. You don't need a degree in finance. You just need the willingness to start. And with Steph as your guide, you are in incredibly capable hands.

Here's to taking the reins. Here's to building the life—and future—you deserve.

Keep shining.

—Kendra Scott

Introduction

One day I had a happy family and a prosperous life. Then suddenly I was alone, sobbing on a park bench and wondering how I'd support my kids. My husband left me and our three sons for a woman with pink hair, 800 cc boobs, and a fondness for gold lamé pants. After 18 years of marriage, I had to start again.

And I did.

Fly! is my story. But if you're reading this book, I am betting that in some ways it might be your story, too.

What happened to me happens to millions of women. According to the Centers for Disease Control and Prevention (CDC), in 2022 alone there were 674,000[1] divorces in the United States, and nearly one million women became widows.[2] And divorce and death aren't the only unexpected events that can turn your world upside down; there are many other ways you can suddenly find yourself out of control of your life and your money—including a job loss, a health crisis, a sudden disability, an economic downturn, unexpected caregiving responsibilities, and even a global pandemic.

When my husband left, I wasn't quite sure of the balance in our checking account or whether my name was on the deed of our house. Oh, did I mention that before I was a wife and mother of three, I was a vice president of a Boston-based private equity fund? Silly me.

Consider this: The average age of widowhood is a surprisingly young 59, and more than half of us will eventually divorce. In fact, the divorce rate for people over 50 has doubled in the last 30 years, and for those over 65, it's tripled.[3] We're also living longer than ever—some of us well into our 90s. All of this means that 80 percent of women will eventually face life alone.[4] And most of us will not be prepared for the financial fallout.

When a woman becomes unexpectedly single, her household income drops by as much as 40 percent, which is more than twice as much as a man's declines.[5] Eighty percent of custodial parents are mothers, which means less income to cover their children's needs. Child support? Don't count on it! Only 45 percent of parents receive the full amount owed.[6]

Nearly 50 percent of women ages 55 to 66 have no retirement savings.[7] We also receive only 80 percent of the Social Security benefits that men collect.[8] Both of these challenges stem largely from lower pay and significant gaps in our lifetime earnings. Some, like me, step off the career path to care for young or disabled kids; others take time off to assist aging parents. And making up for the lost retirement savings and income potential can be nearly impossible. The income issue is compounded for women of color. Today, Black women make just 63 cents for every dollar earned by a white man. It's worse for Latina women, who earn just over half (57 cents) of what white men do.[9]

Add to that the fact that over half of us still defer the financial planning and investment decisions to our partners, and it's no wonder that most of us are ill-prepared to take charge of our finances. Sometimes we voluntarily hand over the financial reins to our partners, and sometimes our partners grab them from us. Here's what's especially shocking: Married millennials are deferring these decisions at a higher rate than any other generation.[10]

Yet, despite all this, many financial institutions continue to assume that the needs of men and women are the same. Some engage in "pink washing"—using marketing tactics that patronize women rather than empower them. The industry further complicates matters with jargon that confuses more than it clarifies. But trust me, there's no shame in not knowing industry lingo. Smart people with smart ideas speak simply—and should.

Additionally, and more importantly, many financial institutions fail to recognize that women's emotional connection to being in charge of their finances can be challenging—often triggering anxiety, stress, and a deeply rooted sense of inadequacy. A 2017 Fidelity Investments survey found that women are less confident than men when it comes to investing, with only 9 percent believing they can outperform their male counterparts.[11]

And why should any of this surprise us? Until 1974, banks could legally deny women credit, require a male cosigner, or charge women higher interest because of their gender,[12] and before 1981, husbands had unilateral control of jointly owned property.[13] Is it any wonder, then, that the belief we are inherently less competent with money has been engrained in our psyches?

When women who may not previously have had to deal with their own finances suddenly find themselves needing to take control, it can be frightening. We judge ourselves for not knowing enough. We feel ashamed and fear other people will find out how naive we are in this area of our lives. Even women who most others would think are self-assured and competent—*Oh, she's an attorney, she knows what she's doing*—may not be, at all. I know women who have created multimillion-dollar businesses who don't feel confident with their personal finances. Remember: Just because you can create wealth doesn't mean you know what to do with it once it hits your bank account.

I care about women owning their financial power because I know what's it's like to lose it. Before becoming a full-time wife and mother, I had a thriving career in finance and a goal of attending Harvard Business School. Then, when I was six months pregnant and had a two-year-old at home, I was asked to board a four-seater Cessna to check out a deal in rural Alabama. I knew something had to give. My husband traveled over

150 nights a year. One of us had to be home. The very next day, I quit. I put my career on hold and, despite my financial aptitude, eventually left all money matters to my husband. What I did not realize then, as a young mom and madly-in-love wife, was that these choices also caused me to relinquish my independence and become a passive observer in my eventual financial downfall.

Thirteen years later I found myself divorced, jobless, and a single mother of three.

My remorse was exacerbated by my loss of purpose and an urgent need to regain my financial independence. I remember thinking, *What am I going to do with the rest of my life? How in the hell will I be able to support my kids after being out of the workforce for 13 years?* But I also knew I didn't have a choice. I had to re-create my life and restart my career because the alternative was too bleak to contemplate—54 percent of older women can't afford to pay for their basic needs.[14] I was not going to become one of those women.

And after you read this book . . . neither will you.

Regaining my economic security was one of the hardest challenges I've ever faced. I stumbled countless times before finding my way back to happiness, self-respect, and financial stability. But as painful as the experience was, it ultimately became a gift that transformed the trajectory of my life.

In the midst of it all, I couldn't help but wonder, *If I, with my financial background, feel this lost and overwhelmed, how must women without that same knowledge feel when thrown into similar circumstances? How many women, unknowingly, are making the same mistakes I did—setting themselves up for future devastation? And, most importantly, how can I help women understand the urgent need to take control of their financial future—right now, long before a crisis ever strikes?*

This became my life's mission.

I took the lessons I learned during that difficult time and added my financial expertise with a newfound unwavering passion for educating and empowering women to take charge of their money. This journey led me to build a national consulting business as a divorce financial strategist, specializing in helping women who find themselves unexpectedly single—particularly those who were the "nonfinancial" spouse: the one who wasn't in charge of the money and now must navigate her financial life on her own. I then went on to build an educational platform that has helped thousands of women across the country expand their financial literacy.

Seven years later, I became the National Director of Women & Wealth at Northern Trust, one of the largest and most respected financial institutions in the world. Today, I lead the firm's advisory practice for women and oversee all creation of content, curriculum, and programming through its Elevating Women platform.

By the time you get to Northern Trust, you already have considerable resources. But no matter how much money you have or don't have, here's what *every* woman needs to know: If you're not used to dealing with your own money, it doesn't matter whether you've got $2,000 or $20 million—many of the emotional challenges are the same. You fear making the wrong move. You trust yourself too little or others too much. If you have less than you're used to, you're scared about how you'll manage. If you have more than you're used to, you may worry about the additional responsibility and whether you're up to the job.

When you're living in fear and avoidance, it's hard to think beyond money. But once you conquer that fear, you gain control of not only your finances but also the direction of your life. And as you move toward living a more genuine and meaningful life, your options and opportunities begin to multiply exponentially.

I can't make you rich, and I can't make you an investment genius. But if you follow the simple lessons in this book, I can help you feel more confident with your finances, better prepared to make big decisions, and finally liberated to make the most of life's many chapters. *Fly!* will prepare you for whatever comes your way.

I'll walk you through the exact steps I took to rebuild my life—both financially and emotionally. This step-by-step process is a road map to help you improve your relationship with money, better understand your current financial landscape, and discover how to make more confident decisions around your wealth. You'll learn how to set transformative goals, craft a comprehensive plan to turn your vision into reality, cultivate an empowering and supportive network, and discover how financial independence can enhance your relationships and unlock exciting new possibilities you never imagined.

But first, I will begin by telling you my story because, in many ways, it is so achingly typical. If a financially savvy person like me could lose complete control over her money, it could happen to anyone. I have worked with brilliant women, respected in their fields, who had no idea what was going on with their own finances until disaster struck. I knew one physician, a top neurologist at a major New York hospital, who only realized she was broke when her wealth advisor called and asked, "Do you know what your husband is doing?" (She had $200,000 in credit card debt and hadn't noticed.) Another woman, an esteemed author, lost all her money not once but twice—that second chance she gave her husband just didn't work out. He was trying to keep up with her success and thought racking up a secret six-figure debt to make up for his lost income was a good idea. They got divorced but not before he asked, "Don't I get some credit? At least I didn't have an affair with some intern."

"At least if you did that, this all would have made sense!" she shot back.

But this book isn't just for those whose worlds have been turned upside down by divorce, widowhood, or financial crises. I hope my story and the lessons I share serve as a wake-up call for every woman—no matter your age, background, or life circumstances. Whether you're in your 20s or 60s, single or married, juggling multiple responsibilities as a mother, retired, or just starting your career, this is your call to action: I want each and every one of you to recognize the critical importance of financial independence.

It's not just about avoiding hardship; it's about feeling prepared for whatever life throws your way—both the good and the bad. It's about shifting from a reactive mindset to a proactive one, especially when it comes to financial literacy. It's about seizing opportunities, pursuing dreams, and living life boldly—on our own terms.

But this will only happen when we stop seeing ourselves as victims and stop telling ourselves worn-out narratives like "I suck at math," "This is my husband's job," or "I'm bad with money."

Before you can elevate yourself, you must stop putting yourself down. At the same time, you must stop saying it's someone else's job to fix your situation. It's not. It's yours. You want to make the most of your life? Own it—including your financial independence.

So, what is financial independence? First let me tell you what it's not. It is not about obtaining a specific account balance, having a particular net worth, or knowing you have enough money to never work again. Financial independence comes from taking responsibility for creating, building, and defending your worth. It is about owning your life and realizing that no one—not your spouse, not your parents, not your friend or boss or lover—can protect and grow your wealth better than you. If you believe—with absolute certainty—that you can handle whatever comes your way, you can become focused, resourceful, and persistent, and you will attain financial freedom even in the face of obstacles.

That's not just a goal; that's your future.

Part One

My Wake-Up Call to Financial Independence

Chapter One

The Last Day of My "Perfect" Life

June 11, 2010, was the last day of my "perfect" life—the only life I had known for nearly 20 years. Summer break had just begun for my three sons, which meant that I was beyond exhausted by 9 p.m. I plopped down on our oversized sofa with a glass of red wine in one hand and the cable remote in the other. My husband, whom I'll call Richard, grabbed a glass, too, and we snuggled up to watch a movie together. It was called *Up in the Air*—ironically, about a traveling salesman with a black American Airlines Concierge Key card who was involved with a married woman.

As the movie ended, Richard turned to me without saying a word. It was clear something in the story had unsettled him. Never in our 18-year marriage had I questioned his faithfulness, but the shifty look in his eyes at that moment made me feel like he was hiding something. Reluctantly, I asked, "Is there someone else?"

And there it was: a quiet yes.

I collapsed to the floor. I could not form a single word—only a scream of disbelief and despair. He was my partner, my lover, my everything. In an instant, everything I thought was, was not—and everything

I thought would be, would never be. My best friend suddenly became a stranger.

I raced up the steps to our bedroom, buried myself under the comforter, and sobbed uncontrollably. Scenes from the past 20 years flashed before me. Our story had the fairytale beginning from the day we met at a college party to the day, several years later, when he proposed at the foot of a roller coaster. His tears of joy as he said his vows to me at our wedding, the thrill when we brought each of our three sons home from the hospital, how we beamed with pride as we built our first home.

Together—and from literally nothing—we had created a life that most can only dream about.

Just two weeks earlier, over dinner, Richard had reassured our middle son, Cole, whose best friend's parents were in the midst of a nasty divorce, that he "never, ever" had to worry about that happening to us. But he had not stopped there. He went on to tell our sons how he hoped they would be lucky and patient enough to find a wonderful woman to spend their life with—just like he had.

I had assumed that woman was me.

Like all marriages, of course, we had our share of challenges. Given Richard's intense travel schedule, raising three boys essentially on my own was utterly exhausting. By the time Friday night arrived, it often took all my energy just to crawl into bed. Any parent of young children knows what it's like to be touched constantly, and by the end of each day, I wished I had a force field around me so I could deflect all those tiny hands. In my state of "too much touch," physical intimacy became more of a chore than a pleasure. But doesn't this happen to all young parents? I believed this was just a stage—a temporary pause for both of us amid the demands of daily life.

I spent the next hour staring into darkness. As I struggled to process how and why this happened, I began to consider my part in the mess. Perhaps I was oblivious to the warning signs. I suppose I put our kids' needs in front of my husband's one too many times. Or maybe we weren't having enough sex. I threw off the covers, got out of bed, and headed back downstairs. Richard was spread out across the sofa with his arms crossed over his face. The only light in the room was from the stars, which were shining bright. I walked over and climbed on top of him. He then lowered his arms and, as he hugged me tightly, said, "Thank you, God."

I wiped the tears from his face and calmly replied, "Let's fix this."

• • •

Infidelity happens for specific reasons or for none at all. But I would argue that the way we deal with betrayal and other types of traumas—as well as all the emotional and financial issues that go with them—almost inevitably can be traced back to our childhoods. Certainly, this was the case for Richard and me. Maybe we were searching for a happily-ever-after more than most.

We met at the University of Southern California (USC), but Richard wasn't your typical private school rich kid like many of our classmates. His mother became pregnant with him at 18 and ended up marrying his father less than a year later. Unsurprisingly, she was soon a single mom. Richard had three fathers by the time he was 10. The second one left in the middle of the night.

He never saw that man again.

By the age of 15, Richard was essentially raising himself. And from the stories I heard, it appeared the only thing Richard and his mother had in common were their beautiful brown eyes. Richard was president of his senior class and a self-proclaimed conservative; his mother, on the other hand, was a free-spirited Dutch immigrant who gleefully extolled the merits of socialism. Despite their differences, Richard adored his mother. He recognized, and deeply appreciated, the sacrifices she made as a young mother in the heart of the South during the late 1960s. Her decision to keep him certainly was not the popular choice. He was more of a friend and, eventually, more like a father to her than a son.

After graduating high school, Richard had a full ride to the University of Texas. But his ambitions extended far beyond the Lone Star State. So, he packed up his car in August 1987 and headed west to LA. Richard worked multiple jobs throughout college to help subsidize USC's $30,000-a-year undergraduate tuition. His mother and stepdad number three did the best they could to help, but $100 a month didn't make much of a dent. So along with his diploma came nearly $100,000 in student loans and credit card debt. And while his fraternity brothers drove shiny new BMWs that their rich daddies paid for with cash, Richard drove a 20-year-old Volvo P1800 that lacked working brakes and a door handle.

I not only did not care but admired him immensely for it. Even at that age, I recognized the value of tenacity and the benefits that come from making it on your own.

I was born in Rockford, Illinois, a city in the Rust Belt most notable for its output of heavy machinery, hardware, and tools. Both my grandfathers worked in factories, and each built their homes with their bare hands. I remember at my wedding, surrounded by friends from USC and a world of privilege, when my grandfather pulled me aside and asked, "Don't you know any bricklayers?" Although he was proud of my parents' upward mobility, my work ethic, and all I had accomplished up to that point, this was his way of reminding me to never forget my roots and the values he taught me. God, I miss that man.

Like both of my grandfathers, Richard was resilient and enterprising. And although he had a strong bond with his mother, he did not exactly have a firm grasp of what it was to be a father and husband. After all, he'd seen all the men in his life cut and run.

When I met Richard, I fell hard, but I wasn't at all interested in a serious relationship. I had big dreams of my own: Wall Street, an Ivy League graduate school, and then the cover of *Forbes*. I had absolutely no desire to *ever* get married. Given my parents' relationship and all I'd witnessed growing up, I thought I'd have to be insane to want that. As a little girl, I spent endless nights peering out my bedroom window, praying that God would help me save my mother and build a cocoon around me, woven with silk strands of hope and dreams. Because outside of this imaginary cocoon, I rarely felt safe. Our home was filled with screaming and fear. The highs were so high, but the lows were even lower.

My mom was more like a sister than a parent—sound familiar? As an only child, I found in her a confidante, a best friend, and a partner in crime, defending ourselves against the enemy—my father—day after day, night after night. We didn't want witnesses to our lives, so few outsiders were ever allowed into our home. Not even my grandparents knew the truth of how we lived. Family dinners were spent in silence, and talking was rarely permitted. We ate on TV tables and watched reruns of *M*A*S*H* and *The Dick Van Dyke Show*. That is, when meals weren't thrown onto the floor.

Everything had to be perfect.

Undercooked French fries or pizza cut into uneven pieces would cause my father to fly into a rage. My dad was determined to control every aspect of my mom's world—from the money she spent and the clothes she wore (jeans were not allowed, skirts preferred) to how and with whom she spent her time. My mother was an intelligent and highly successful woman, yet she was too frightened to leave. He threatened to destroy her career, leave her in financial ruin, and even kill her. His ultimatums paralyzed her. Appeasing him seemed like her only choice. Consequently, I was determined to become independent, both financially and emotionally. And I vowed never to allow *any* man to change that—and I stuck to it.

Until the day I met a certain Southern boy.

From our first kiss on the steps of Von KleinSmid Center in the middle of campus to our first "I love you" at Gladstones, a beachside restaurant in Malibu, Richard and I were inseparable. I no longer envisioned my future—I pictured *our* future. My dream of working on Wall Street was quickly replaced by working as an analyst at an investment bank in West LA—admittedly a tall order since there were only a few. But I did it. I became one of two hires out of 1,250 candidates at Jefferies & Co., off Santa Monica Boulevard. My compensation package in 1992: a $10,000 signing bonus, $60,000 base salary, another $60,000 as a guaranteed bonus, and a straight shot to Harvard Business School.

Just one year earlier, Richard's search for his first job hadn't been quite as successful. As a business major with an emphasis in real estate, his sights were set on becoming a commercial broker at a top firm. But the economic downturn that racked California in the early 1990s made getting a job in that industry virtually impossible. So, Richard did what he did best: He pivoted quickly and found the first job he could, selling phone systems to small businesses.

His base salary was just $14,000 a year. So he put two suits, two ties, and two dress shirts on a credit card and set off to build a career. To cover his exorbitant credit card and student loan debt, he slept on a futon in the corner of his biological father's 900-square-foot apartment in Marina del Rey. On the outside, Richard wore a huge smile and exuded optimism to everyone he encountered, but with me it was different. We would regularly sit inside my car in the parking lot of his dad's apartment, where he would sob.

This wasn't how he envisioned things when he left Texas four years earlier. Despite having a job, he had no money for food, clothes, gasoline, or insurance. He was worried that he would lose everything before he even had anything. But then the grit that had defined Richard since he was a boy would resurface and conquer his self-doubt. After every setback, he'd come back to say, "No matter what, no one can take my degree from me."

Just after my graduation day in June 1992, Richard proposed to me at Disneyland, with the diamond from one of his mother's three previous wedding rings. "Life is a roller coaster with fast times and slow times, with steep climbs and great falls," he said as we headed up the first ascent inside the walls of Space Mountain. As we started our initial descent, he yelled, "Will you marry me?"

"Yes!" I shouted back.

So now I had *two* reasons to be screaming on the roller coaster.

Three years later we left Southern California and moved to Texas. I had bypassed graduate school and landed a great job at a Boston-based private equity fund, and I was now opening their Texas office. Richard's career had taken off, too. After about a year of selling phones, he persuaded a guy who was raising money for an equipment-leasing limited partnership to take a chance on him. It didn't take long before he proved his ability to raise some serious cash, and at just 28 he became vice president of a mutual fund company. That same year, our first son, Dillon, was born. Richard and I were true partners in every sense—our lives, our work, and our finances. We earned together, managed our money together, set goals as a team, and worked side by side to achieve them. We had it all: a beautiful family, a 5,000-square-foot home on five acres just outside of Austin, and two flourishing careers in finance.

That was, until that day I was asked to board a Cessna and fly to WhereTheHellAmI, Alabama, to look at a company—an investment opportunity for the fund. I was never wild about flying, but the thought of a bumpy ride in a four-seater plane gave me serious pause. With an almost two-year-old at home and a baby in my belly, the thought of risking my life and leaving my toddler motherless further deepened my distaste. I wanted a career, but I wanted my kids to have a full-time mother more. So, with Richard's full support, I quit.

Not once did I think twice about what I was giving up—my earning power, my independence, and one of the most coveted careers in finance. In fact, looking back, I realize the worst thing my boss—and the founder of the private equity firm—said to me was, "Steph, you will *always* have a job here." Although those words were meant to comfort me, they gave me a false sense of security that what I was giving up would be just as easy to get back. At the time, what mattered most to me was doing what I believed was best for our children.

In fact, Richard and I were both determined to create the perfect family life, and for two people from such fractured, fraught families, that meant a happy road warrior dad and a full-time, hands-on mom. And I would approach child-rearing with the same ferocity and focus I applied to my career. It wasn't even money that we needed to give them. Richard and I were going to give our kids the baseball, apple pie, *Leave It to Beaver*-esque American life we always wished we'd had.

And for a while, we did.

• • •

Not even the sound of my alarm could pry my eyes open that next morning. I had hoped I would wake up to find that this was all just a horrendous dream. But this nightmare was my new reality, and unfortunately, the physical reminders—my swollen eyes and exhausted face—would fade far sooner than the wounds of my shattered heart.

I just laid there, staring at the ceiling unable to escape the image of him with her. How could Richard have done this to me? Questions swirled in my head, each one a fresh stab of pain. How did they meet? How long had the affair been going on? What did she look like? What type of mother was she? (Oh yeah, I learned the night before that she had a family, too.) Did she work? Was she everything I wasn't—successful, carefree, exciting? The person who had just shattered my life was a complete stranger.

My imagination took over. An image of this woman began to take shape: cascading hair, emerald-green eyes, and a gaze that gleamed with confidence. This woman wore a tailored red dress that hugged her curves perfectly, and a pair of matching pumps accentuated her long legs. A diamond necklace glinted around her neck, and a designer handbag hung from her arm. She spent her days volunteering at her child's school, sitting on philanthropic boards, lunching with prominent women in her community—all while juggling a fabulous career.

I hated her. And I could not reconcile how a married man—*my husband*, who went to daily mass and reconciliation each week (now I know why!)—could covet her.

If Richard was so unhappy, didn't he have an obligation to at least tell me? Isn't honesty the foundation of marriage? Isn't it an essential part of the commitment you make when you take each other's hand—the hand of your best friend—on your wedding day as you promise to love each other today, tomorrow, and forever? It's the hand that you expect to hold as you walk alongside each other, chasing your dreams and building a future together. It's the hand that is there to wipe tears of sorrow and joy from your eyes, without judgment or reservation. And it's the hand that you count on to help you care for your family and hold you tight as you struggle through this difficult thing called life. So, what happened that caused Richard to shit on this commitment and to completely disregard the feelings of not only our family but also the other family he was destroying? It wasn't just about me and my boys. His mistress had a daughter and a husband whose lives had changed forever as well, whether they knew it yet or not.

Still in bed, I heard the slam of the front door. I suddenly remembered that it was no ordinary day. Our rising sixth grader was off to Boy Scout camp. For the last week, preparation had been in full force, and Cole was beaming with excitement. Despite the fact that our family was now in shambles, life had to go on. I needed to dig deep inside my soul and find a way to pull myself together and maintain as much normalcy as possible for my sons. Richard had made a mess out of their lives—just like my father had done to mine—and once again, it would become my responsibility to clean it up. I grabbed my robe, put on a fake smile, and headed downstairs to say goodbye.

Richard greeted me at the bottom of the stairwell with a kiss on the forehead and a whisper: "I promise I will call her and end it."

"Please do, Richard," I whispered back. "Tell her to stay the hell out of our lives. Tell her that you are done with this crap! Please!"

We had so much to talk about and work through, but for now, this would be Richard's first step toward building a bridge back to my heart. He assured me he would end things with her and headed out the door.

My wide-eyed, optimistic Cole, with a heart as big as Texas, ran outside but quickly turned and rushed back in for a hug before the door could even shut. As he squeezed me tight, he uttered, "Bye, Mom, I love you!"

The squeeze of his little arms filled me with love and brought a genuine grin to my face. "I love you, too, buddy. You have no idea how much I am going to miss you. Have fun, and I will see you next week."

Cole raced out the door with the same enthusiasm he'd shown when he ran in, and just like that—*poof*—I was alone again, facing day one of my new normal. I headed up the stairs and slithered back into bed, seeking refuge under my fluffy down comforter. A pool of tears welled up in my eyes again, until exhaustion finally overcame me. I drifted into a shallow sleep.

Suddenly, my cell phone rang. It was Richard. "Cole's having sharp pains in his stomach. It's probably nerves. You know how much anxiety he gets when he leaves home. What should I do?"

Richard had always been the "fun" parent—the one who took the boys hunting, fishing, and camping and on all kinds of exciting adventures. Nurturing their aches and pains, or soothing their wounded hearts, had always been my job. So, I wasn't surprised by his uncertainty when it came to dealing with Cole's bellyache.

"Go ahead and take him to camp, just make sure to let the nurse know. We're just a few hours away, and I will go get him if his symptoms get worse," I replied.

Meanwhile, I could hear Dillon and Drew in the next room, laughing and playing—just as young boys should. Their voices, light and carefree, soothed my mind like a gentle rain on a tin roof. Slowly I began to drift back to sleep.

The phone rang again, and as I scrambled to grab my cell, I caught a glimpse of the time. What had felt like a short nap had turned into a deep sleep, and just like that, several hours had passed.

"Mrs. Wagner? This is Sue, the nurse up here at Bear Creek. I have Cole with me. He's complaining of sharp pains in his lower left side. I'm worried it might be appendicitis."

I panicked and frantically dialed Richard. "The nurse thinks Cole needs surgery! We have to get him to a hospital!" Throwing off my robe, I sprang out of bed, my voice hoarse. "Hurry, guys—get dressed! We need to meet Dad and Cole. It's serious!"

My heart pounded as I raced downstairs. I grabbed my purse and a pair of oversized sunglasses to hide my tear-streaked cheeks, and within minutes, the three of us were in our SUV, heading up the interstate to a regional hospital located halfway between home and camp.

As I looked down the long stretch of highway, my mind raced. Although I was sick with worry for Cole, I couldn't stop thinking about Richard's infidelity. How long had I been sharing my husband? What intimate secrets about me were now in the hands of my new enemy? I wanted to puke.

At what point did my life become a lie?

I didn't even know her name. In fact, I knew hardly anything about her, except for the fact that she thought it was acceptable to have sex with my husband. I can only imagine the fantasies they played out as they wined and dined, all while I was at home washing his nasty underwear. Wouldn't every woman love the opportunity to escape their daily routine and endless responsibilities for a night of passion and mind-blowing sex? But the commitment I made nearly 20 years earlier, and again when I chose to bring three children into this world, prevented me from ever making *that* a reality. I was engulfed by anger. As hard as I tried to focus on Cole and his possible appendectomy, I was fixated on the deadly disease my family contracted called the pink-haired lady—the name I would eventually unaffectionately give her.

As I pulled into the hospital, I spotted Richard's Ford F350 truck parked recklessly near the ER entrance. While I raced inside to join them, Dillon and Drew veered off into the waiting room, their heads buried in their electronic devices. By the time I reached the room, Cole was already being wheeled away on a gurney, headed for a CT scan of his abdomen.

As the door shut behind him and the nurse, I turned to Richard with a mix of urgency and desperation in my voice. "Did you call her? Did you end it? Did you fix this mess?"

His solemn reply landed like a ton of bricks. "I tried," he said, barely above a whisper. "And she's furious I told you."

Wait, *what*? Did she actually think she had a right to be angry?

Oh, how naive I was to think this could be resolved swiftly—like pulling out a splinter with tweezers, quick and painless, leaving no trace. The reality started to sink in; the pink-haired lady wasn't going to just go away. And with 21 years invested in my relationship with Richard, and my three precious boys who depended on both of us, I wasn't ready to let go.

Less than 24 hours had passed since I learned of the affair. My wounds were fresh, raw, and deep. If only I had a glimpse into the future to see how this story would unfold, I would have kicked Richard's ass to the curb without a second thought. But life doesn't offer previews, nor does the full truth of any traumatic event reveal itself all at once. And I was left grappling with the painful uncertainty about all of what lay ahead.

Chapter Two
Rinse and Repeat

Looking in the mirror six weeks after Richard's confession, I almost didn't recognize myself. I was emaciated, weighing barely over 100 pounds. My eyes were sunken, and my hair was dull.

Our impending summer vacation sounded perfect in theory: a two-week family trip up the East Coast, filled with museums, sightseeing, and quality time for the five of us. But as the departure date grew nearer, my anxiety overshadowed my anticipation. I clung to the illusion that this getaway would be what Richard and I needed to finally get back on track. But the reality was that I was failing miserably at trying to create normalcy for the boys. Even the thought of sitting next to Richard on a plane and then staying in a 20-by-15-foot hotel room for two weeks was suffocating.

As our plane ascended, I caught an aerial view of our neighborhood and immediately felt a steady flow of tears running down my cheeks. Our home, which had once contained so much love, now felt like a tomb. We barely spoke, and my desperate appeals for love and support were met with resistance. Sex is often the Hail Mary in failing marriages, so we were having lots of it. But it was emotionless and unsatisfying for me, and each time it was over, I felt more and more alone. The confidence I once exuded was replaced by insecurity and submissiveness. I had become a stranger—not only to myself, but also to the friends and family who knew the torment I was living through. They pleaded with me to leave Richard and restore my dignity, but I ignored them all.

My head knew what I needed to do, but my heart refused to listen. I couldn't let go of the past—everything we had built together and all the dreams we had yet to accomplish. To make things worse, I was now completely financially dependent on Richard. Despite my love for finance and my skill set, I had no idea how we were spending our money, what our balances looked like, or how much debt we had. I had no grasp of where assets were invested or even the details of our retirement plan. The demands of running a household, raising children, and subsequent division of duties between Richard and I had created these blind spots. I hadn't willingly handed over control of our money nor had Richard intentionally taken it from me. Life just happened. And now I was starting to face the consequences of that.

I reached for Richard, who sat next to me in first class while our three boys sat together back in the main cabin. Richard was accustomed to the American Airlines black card, first-class-only, Master of the Universe lifestyle. Flying as a family, we had only two upgrades available, and Richard wasn't about to give up his free cocktails and warm bowl of nuts just so we could all sit together.

I turned to him. "Do you love me?" I asked.

"I will tell you I love you when I want to tell you I love you," he said. He pulled his hand away and buried his head back in his *Wall Street Journal.* "Please, Richard, talk to me! I forgive you. I just want to talk and understand why you did this. How could you do this to our family?" I couldn't stop picking at the wound.

He threw down his paper and hissed, "You're crazy. You are a fucking nut!"

I began to sob. What had I done to deserve this? The more I tried to show love and forgiveness, the more contempt he showed me. The next 40 minutes of our flight were interminable.

As we pulled into the gate, Richard shoved his paper into his brief-case, stood up, and regarded me coldly. "I refuse to sit with you on the next leg of our flight—you're a mess!"

Before I could respond, he was out the door of the plane. As I waited for the boys to exit, I slid my sunglasses down onto my face hoping that would be enough to hide my swollen eyes. The three of them leaped with excitement down the aisle after having to sit still for an hour and greeted me with a huge smile. We spent a five-hour weather delay in the Admirals Club, an hour-and-a-half waiting on the tarmac, and three hours on another flight before finally arriving in Washington, DC. By now it was nearly midnight, and hunger and exhaustion had set in for everyone. We hustled to get our bags and found our driver holding a sign with WAG-NER in big bold letters.

For all of those hours, there was virtual silence. I felt more like hired help than a wife. Was I here simply to take care of our kids? Shortly after 1 a.m., we arrived at our hotel. And as the doors to the elevator shut, pain shot down my arms and my skin began to ache. I had never felt anything like this before. It was as if my flesh was turning inside out, and with every passing second, it intensified. Every breath became harder and harder to take, and my chest began to tighten.

I panicked. "I can't do this!" I yelled, as tears streamed down my cheeks again. My children just stood there. I couldn't stop myself from crying, and I couldn't say anything more. I felt paralyzed. The next thing I remember was being hand in hand with Dillon as we lay next to each other in one of the room's queen beds. Drew and Cole were together in the other while Richard slept on a rollaway in the far corner of the room.

I was the first to wake that next morning, and as I rose to my feet, I thought I might just crumble to the ground. I was already slim, a runner; I couldn't afford to lose five pounds, let alone 15. But here I was. I had been trying to avoid mirrors, and seeing myself at that moment was devastating. When I learned the man I had built a life around had been having an affair—one that, I would later find out, had lasted two and a half years—I could no longer eat. I struggled with sleep. I had lost my capacity for joy.

It's ironic, really. I had the marriage that could actually be problematic—it made friends jealous. And, frankly, it caused issues with their husbands (Richard's friends), when their wives complained to them about how they needed to be more "attentive like Richard." Be careful what you wish for. I'd tell friends stories about Richard—how he'd fly home from a business trip only to leave again the next morning just to spend extra time with me and the boys, how I had admired a little black dress in the window of a boutique up the street and come home a few days later to find it slung over a chair in our bedroom—and they would ooh and ahh, saying I couldn't possibly understand the problems in *their* marriages.

And why shouldn't I boast about Richard? I thought at the time. Look how much he was sacrificing to put our kids in great private schools, give us the home we wanted, and give me the freedom to be the stay-at-home mom I (we) felt they deserved. It wasn't just that we'd come a long way financially. That was true and wonderful. But the real journey, or the journey that thrilled me the most, was that we'd both escaped the wreckage of our childhoods. We were *not* our parents. Instead, we were creating the life for our children that we always wanted to have.

That's what I thought. That's what I craved.

I studied my gaunt figure in the bathroom mirror.

I had always greeted life with exclamation points. I actually kind of enjoyed obstacles for the sheer pleasure of knowing I could leap over them. But this time was different. I was becoming the type of woman I had spent years pitying and—if I'm being brutally honest—judging. They were the mothers of my children's friends, wives of my husband's business associates, women who seemed to have lost themselves in the identity of their husbands, going through the motions each day and replacing their dreams, talents, and ideas with someone else's.

How had I become one of them in just six short weeks?

Just then, I noticed Dillon standing beside me. In a soft yet stern voice he said, "Stop letting him do this to you." He hugged me tight. He was 12.

That day, roaming the nation's capital with the temperature hovering in the 90s, the tension only got worse. Sweltering, we waited in long lines to visit one museum after another, forcing laughs and faking smiles. The seemingly effortless cheer of other families around me ate me up inside. I found myself creating stories about them. Happy families! But maybe they weren't. Were they as miserable as we were? There's something about forced fun that can feel like an anvil around your neck.

By 4 p.m. I needed a drink. There was a small café next to our hotel, so trying to sound relaxed, I asked Richard, "How about some vino and a bite to eat?" Enticing Richard with wine was easy, so it was no surprise when he replied, "Yes, most definitely, but I need to stop by the hotel first and take care of a few things."

The boys and I waited in the lobby while Richard headed up to the room. I wasn't exactly sure what "business" he had to tend to. When Richard returned, something had changed. His shifting eyes made me anxious. "Let's go," Richard ordered sharply. The boys and I obediently followed.

I snapped. "Richard, stop. What the hell is your problem? You've been ignoring me all day. This is ridiculous, especially in front of our kids. I haven't done anything to you. We need to talk—now!"

"Fine," he shot back and proceeded to leave the hotel and walk over to the adjacent park.

Cole hustled to my left side and grabbed my hand tightly. I reached with my right hand and clasped Drew's little fingers, and together the three of us scurried across the street. Dillon marched beside us, like a trainer alongside a boxer just before he enters the ring to fight.

Together, my sons and I huddled on a long wooden park bench while Richard loomed over us. His eyes were empty. And before I could utter a word, Richard blurted, "I am moving to the ranch. Your mom and I are not happy. We decided this is best for everyone."

I sat there, stunned. *We* hadn't decided anything. *We* had never even discussed it. Telling the boys that Daddy was moving to the ranch—our second home and the house *I* designed—wasn't what I had in mind when I called this meeting. And oh, by the way, our "ranch" consisted of two longhorn steers named Oreo and Bevo.

Good, I thought. *Go rot at the ranch with the cows. Swim with the water moccasins and cow shit infesting our pond.*

Was this really happening? Did he really just tell our kids in the middle of a strange city in 95-degree heat that he was leaving? I wanted to scream, tell him what an ass he was being and what a horrible man he had become. But before I got the chance, he turned his back to us and calmly walked away, leaving me sitting on a park bench in the middle of Washington, DC, 1,500 miles away from home, surrounded by our three young sons.

I had no husband, no cash, and no job. In my purse, there was one credit card and the key to a lonely house.

• • •

Although I never saw this chaos coming, maybe, in some way, I was trained for it. As a child (and later, as an adult), I had watched my mother placate my father and rationalize his grotesque behavior. It was her attempt to have the life she was taught to have by her mother and grandmother. And by all outward appearances—the cars in the garage, the home with the manicured lawn, a successful real estate career, and a loving daughter, son-in-law, and three beautiful grandsons—she did. But she secretly lived through hell. Until one day in September 2002 when she decided she'd had enough.

It was a sunny morning—Friday the 13th, in fact—when my father opened the garage, pulled out in his Mercedes, and descended the steep driveway toward the exit of their gated neighborhood. He had planned to squeeze in a few errands and a quick lunch with my mom before heading to the country club for a round of golf with his buddies. To my father's surprise, his lunch date would be an off-duty sheriff, serving him divorce papers and a protective order signed by a county judge that very day.

Just a few days prior, I had received a call from my mom. The panic in her voice was something I had recognized many times as a child, but I hadn't heard it in a while. I had grown so frustrated and exhausted by my mother's failed attempts to break the cycle of abuse that I had distanced myself, even though now we lived only a mile apart. But this phone call felt different. My mother was hiding in her office, whispering. She couldn't talk loudly or for long.

On the previous night, she told me, my father had awakened and gone looking for her after realizing that she was missing from their bed. He went upstairs to find my mom curled up on the floor of her office with a small pillow and blanket. Still half-asleep, she found herself being dragged down a flight of stairs. He pulled her by her hair and threw her back into bed. The abuse I witnessed as a child had escalated, and she was at her breaking point. I had waited over three decades for this moment—one of few kids who actually prayed for a broken home.

The next morning, I sprang into action. We needed the best attorney in town, the one who would take her seriously. Mom and I found ourselves in the office of Terry Weeks, an older, heavyset man who was definitely a member of the Texas good ole boys' club. His jeans were starched nearly as much as his dress shirt, and his cowboy hat was displayed on the coatrack that stood next to the credentials and awards that covered every inch of his office wall. He was confident without being patronizing or intimidating; his seasoned expression said he had seen it all.

"What can I do for you?" Weeks sat down, pen in hand, prepared to document our life stories. It didn't take long for him to realize that this was no ordinary meeting, and there was much more to it than a simple, "Sir, we are here to learn how to file for divorce." Weeks pushed his writing pad aside and sat back in his chair. "Tell me, Eve, what are you afraid of?"

After a long pause, the truth began to flow. My mom told story after story, including being submerged under water in their hot tub and being locked out of hotel rooms without a stitch of clothing on. Once, as a form of punishment, my father forced her to stand butt-ass naked in front of a large picture window for all the neighbors to see. The half hour she stood on display must have seemed like an eternity. She described incident after incident, quickly and without much emotion, almost as if she were reading a grocery list.

Weeks thought for a moment. Then he leaned forward and folded his hands under his chin. "Eve, may I ask you a question? Have you ever been abused?"

"No, I have never had a black eye or a broken bone," she replied.

He immediately responded, "Ma'am, this is the worst case of abuse I have heard in my 35 years of practicing law."

He explained that given the volatility of the situation, he would need to put a protective order in place (not to be confused with a restraining order, which has little to no enforceability). Once served, this order would prevent my father from being within 500 feet of my mom, my children, or me. If he chose to ignore the order, he would be thrown in jail with no questions asked.

All three of us understood the severity of the situation. We'd all watched enough *Dateline* episodes—and my mother and I certainly had enough personal experience—to predict my father's reaction.

As the meeting ended, my mom said, "Thank you so much for your time. You have been wonderful. I will start planning my exit strategy by getting my affairs in order. I do, however, have a very important business event six weeks from now, which we"—my mother and father—"are hosting together. Immediately after that, I will give you a call."

Old habits die hard.

My mom spent nearly 35 years under my father's controlling influence. So, I guess she thought, *What's the harm in waiting another couple of months?*

Ironically, outside our home, my mother was a force. Before dominating the Austin real estate market, she'd had a successful career as a national fundraiser for nonprofits, working with business and community leaders like Walter Annenberg and Nancy Reagan, and A-list celebrities like Tom Hanks, Rita Wilson, Tom Selleck, and Elizabeth Taylor. In fact, for many years she outearned my father. My mom was the kind of role model any child would be proud of. And yet, every week, she received an allowance. She had no say in how her hard-earned money was spent. My father refused to share any information about their financial situation, she had no idea how much money she had, the debt she was responsible for, or whether she could ever retire. All those years watching her let him degrade and control her overshadowed that pride.

Wait, what? I wanted to shake her and scream, "Are you kidding me? We have come this far, and now you're putting this off for another two months?" It hit me—she might not be alive by then.

Thank God she snapped out of it. It took only another 24 hours under the same roof as my dad before she realized what had to be done, no matter how scared she was.

Screw the business event. The time was now.

She hustled to take care of things on her end, which included sneaking into my dad's desk drawer to steal a check (toward the back of the checkbook so that he would not notice any problems with the number sequence). The check would be made out to J. Terry Weeks in the amount of $7,000. It was a retainer for his services and an investment in a new life.

Weeks was hurrying on his end as well, preparing not only standard divorce documents but also my mother's affidavit, which he and my mom would need to personally present to the judge. Although it had been just 72 hours since she called me, this plan had been in the works for most of my life.

The following Friday, while my dad was running errands before an afternoon of golf, the locks were changed. My mom raced to the courthouse to get in front of a judge, and I dropped Dillon and Cole off at preschool. We planned to meet back at her house by 10:30 a.m., which would allow plenty of time for us to hunker down and wait for my dad. Regardless of what the court order said, we knew that it was only a matter of time before he would ignore it and return to the house.

As I walked through the front door, I caught a whiff of Mr. Clean and heard a vacuum. Amid all the chaos, someone forgot to cancel the cleaning lady. Sweet Mary had been helping my mom for years. And she knew a lot more about my parents' lives than just the color of their underwear. I have little doubt that she witnessed my father's fury firsthand, but she cared for my mother and continued to come every Friday.

Within a few minutes, I heard the garage door open, and my mom walked into the house. She seemed peaceful. Perhaps it was sinking in that my dad would not be coming home that night—or any other night for that matter. Freedom was close, but there was still so much that could go wrong.

We locked all the doors, checked the locks, and checked again. Clutching a phone, we huddled together and waited on the sofa. We had a clear view of the driveway, so we would be able to see his white Mercedes pull up.

I could not stop imagining my father. I saw him sitting in front of Texas Land and Cattle, waiting for my mom to meet him, and inwardly trying to decide between the T-bone or rib eye for lunch. A sheriff sat in an unmarked car, just a few feet away.

It was just before noon when my father pulled up. Shit, we were right. Clearly, a court order couldn't keep a narcissist away. My mom's serenity suddenly turned to fear, and she began to panic. I had a flashback to a day 20 years before, when we locked ourselves in the bathroom with only a flimsy metal lock on a wooden door between us and my screaming, raging father. Like then, in this moment I could barely catch my breath; sharp pains shot down my arms toward the tips of my fingers.

The doorbell rang. There was no pounding or screaming, just a ding-dong. My father stood on the front stoop as if he were an invited guest. All that was missing was the casserole dish and a bottle of wine. As odd as it seems, perhaps this was his way of honoring the order. After all, my dad often made up his own rules. Inside, my mom and I were running in circles. I attempted to dial 9-1-1, but misdialed as my fingers shook. Then, finally, I connected with an emergency operator.

In the midst of all the chaos, Mary continued to mop. Her heart may have stopped a time or two, but she never stopped pushing that mop along the floor. Oh, how I could understand poor Mary: I had assumed that same role for so many years, just pushing my mop and trying to clean the mess my father made of our lives.

After no one answered the door, my dad calmly turned around and got in his car. His calm was in a way more frightening than his rage. By now the police were dispatched and what would happen next was out of our control.

Soon after, my mother's close friend arrived to take over my role for a while, as I still had the responsibilities of my everyday life to tend to. Plus, as frightened as I was, I needed to know where my dad had gone—yet I had no idea where to start. Being trapped in the house only made me feel more helpless. I assured my mom I'd be gone for only a few minutes and explained that I had to run to the bank and make a deposit, which was true. In the interest of saving time, I raced to the nearest grocery store, which had a bank branch inside. I pulled in and parked. As I shut the car door my eyes locked onto a white Mercedes—surrounded by two police cars.

Oh my God. There was my dad, pressed against his car, handcuffed.

It was pure coincidence. I hadn't expected to find him there. In fact, despite my desire to know where he was, I hadn't expected to find him at all.

Instinctively, and almost without emotion, I walked toward him. I will never be able to erase the memory of the expression on his face and the fear in his eyes. He had always been so protected by his money, his privilege, his swagger—and his ability to make the women in his life cower. Now he looked like an abandoned child, wondering who would take care of him. Who would love him? How could someone he loves have done this to him?

Ironically, at that moment, I remembered only the good. I recalled the times my dad would cry over commercials or dance around the house singing the Randy Newman song "I Love LA" or the endless hours he spent commuting to Los Angeles or San Diego from our home in Orange County so that I could go to great schools and be a part of a wonderful community. Or the joy on his face when he surprised me with a new car on my high school graduation day. Or how he beamed with pride when I was accepted to USC. This was my fault. It was me who had made the call. It was me who threw those cuffs on, and it was me who would cause him to spend three nights in the Travis County jail.

The life he had just a few hours earlier? He'd never get it back.

• • •

That night in DC, with the only credit card in my wallet and no idea what the balance or available credit was, I booked a new hotel for me and the kids. It was conveniently located near the train station, which made it an easy walk for our party of four to haul our bulky suitcases. Our next stop: Boston. Months earlier, Richard and I had promised our sons a family vacation, and by God, I was determined to still give them one.

The boys had never been on a train, and despite what they'd been hit with the night before, they were buzzing with excitement the next morning as they boarded and settled into their seats. Raised in Texas, where public transportation is essentially nonexistent, the novelty of a train ride couldn't be beat. It also offered a welcome distraction.

As for me, well, keeping it together was a Herculean effort. Fighting back tears, I forced a smile. "Guys, my stomach is killing me," I fibbed,

"I'll be right back." As I stepped into the vestibule, surrounded by the clatter and bumps, hidden from view and sound, I finally allowed the tears to flow. I paced back and forth, the weight of our situation pressing down on me. And then, with much hesitation and the fear of the inevitable "I told you so," I dialed the number of a close friend whose husband was an attorney back home. I desperately needed emotional support—and some solid legal advice—and I needed both fast. She didn't hesitate. "Book a flight for you and the boys. Get home. Now." Then, she gave me the name of a top divorce attorney and urged me to call immediately.

The train ride to Boston was initially expected to last six to seven hours. But instead, it turned into a grueling 10-hour ordeal—all thanks to a three-hour delay inside Penn Station, where the train stood still on the tracks underground. It was dark and extremely hot. It was close to 10 p.m. by the time we finally got off the train, and all four of us were famished and exhausted.

And as we exited the station, I surveyed the dimly lit taxi pickup area. It was empty—no cars, no people, just an eerie silence. On the outskirts of Boston (in 2010 before the luxury of Uber), I had a chilling realization: We may have just missed our last chance for a ride. Five minutes stretched into 10, and still there was no sign of help. But just as I turned to head back into the station, hoping to find a number to call for assistance, two bright headlights rounded the corner inside the concrete structure. A bright yellow cab pulled up to the curb, and the driver—a young man with a Jamaican accent and a warm smile—stepped out and loaded our bags into his trunk.

The boys eagerly climbed into the back seat, and I slid into the front. And as I fastened my seatbelt, I couldn't help but notice a Bob Marley bobblehead on the dashboard. The animated figure held a small sign that read "Don't worry, be happy." Tears spilled from the corners of my eyes. In that moment, happiness felt like an elusive dream.

Struggling to compose myself, I forced a fake grin and offered the driver the address of our hotel. Although he couldn't possibly know our story, the sight of three young boys traveling late at night with their tearful, sniffling mother likely painted a clear picture. Laid-back Caribbean tunes filled the car as we drove. Sensing our distress, the cab driver began to hum along softly, his warmth a stark contrast to my despair in the darkness of the night. Then, in a compassionate voice, he turned to me and said, "Remember, storms pass, and the sun always rises. It will all be okay."

That kind gentleman was the first of three angels who crossed our paths that night—albeit briefly—and he left an indelible mark on my heart. The other two angels appeared within minutes after we checked into the hotel. By then it was 11:15 p.m.

"Y'all must be starving," I said, waiting at the front desk for our room key. "Dillon, why don't you take your brothers to see what you can order?"

The three of them eagerly rushed over to the bar, where two older women, who were in the middle of cleaning up for the night, turned their attention to them with warm smiles. "I'm sorry, darlings," one of the ladies said, her voice filled with empathy, "but the kitchen closed at eleven." The three of them returned to me. Their disappointment was evident in their slumped shoulders and slow, dragging steps.

Feeling a bit of desperation, I approached the ladies, hoping for some leniency. "We've been traveling all day from DC." I explained, my voice full of exhaustion and emotion. "Our train, which ran out of food, was delayed for almost four hours." Then, lowering my voice so my boys couldn't hear, I confided in the two women. "Last night, in the middle of our family vacation, their dad announced he was moving out. And now, I'm doing everything I can to keep things as normal for them as possible."

"Oh, sweetie, we've got you," one of the ladies said with assurance, her words like a comforting embrace. "Now, go up to the room and get those boys ready for bed, and we will be up in a few."

While the boys were taking turns showering, putting on their pj's, and brushing their teeth, there was a knock on the door. I opened it and stood in disbelief as both women rolled in a separate room service cart, covered with food ranging from caprese salad and chicken wings to French fries, cookies, and fruit. And there, in the far-right corner of the second cart, stood not one but two bottles of red wine. I couldn't help but laugh. "We both thought you needed some of that, maybe even more than the food," they said.

"Indeed," I replied.

I searched for the bill, planning to add an enormous tip, but it couldn't be found. I asked, "Where do I sign?"

"No, it's on us!" one of the women replied. "Consider it a gift. It's just what we as women do for each other."

It was a powerful moment.

Asking for help isn't easy. Too often, as women, we're expected to do it all and maintain an unshakeable facade every step of the way. But that night, in a moment of sheer desperation, I had to swallow my pride and ask for support. And what I received in return was truly life-changing. Those women didn't just feed us; they showered us with kindness and empathy, and they gave me hope.

Despite our differences, there is an unbreakable sisterhood among women. We may come from different backgrounds, hold different beliefs, but deep down, we are connected by a shared understanding: Life throws curveballs, ranging from minor setbacks to major obstacles. Yet regardless of their magnitude, no woman should face them alone. Instead, we need to embrace vulnerability, seek and offer support, and nurture the bonds that unite us as women.

The next morning, I found myself dialing the number of a dear friend, a somewhat ironic twist given that he was the founder (and my former boss) of the private equity firm I left over 13 years earlier. It felt a bit like a full-circle moment, considering that my decision to quit certainly was a contributing factor to the mess I was now in. Over the years, Jim and I remained close friends, and I adored his wife, Robin, who had transitioned to stay-at-home mom to two sons after graduating from Harvard Medical School and starting her own internal medicine practice.

As I recounted what happened back in DC and bits and pieces of the hell I'd been through over the last month, Jim seemed as taken aback as I was. He loved Richard. They, too, were friends, grabbing dinner when their travels coincided in the same city. After learning about my predicament, he immediately shot out, "Steph, Robin and I are heading to the Cape tonight. Come!"

"Are you sure?" I replied.

"Yes, a few days at the beach will be good for the boys, and I think you could use some support right now," he added.

The invitation to their beach house was an offer I couldn't refuse.

Jim was right. The boys needed this, and I did, too. So, after a long day of sightseeing in downtown Boston, which included a stop at the Boston Tea Party Ships and the playgrounds at Boston Common, I secured a rental car, and we set off for Cape Cod.

As darkness fell, Cole and Drew drifted asleep in the back seat. Dillon, perched in the front seat, finally broke the lingering silence between us. It felt as though we were all clinging to an unspoken agreement—a desperate hope that ignoring the events in DC and our journey since would somehow erase them. It was a childish fantasy, like the unspoken code of silence that existed between my mom and me after every one of my father's rampages. I wondered what these boys were thinking, feeling. So far, the only comfort I could offer them was a mantra repeated on autopilot—an empty promise that everything would be okay.

"Mom," he began, his voice small but resolute, "I get it. You're like the giving tree."

I was taken aback by his unexpected metaphor. The giving tree? What did he mean?

"You know," he continued, his voice gaining strength, "like in the story. 'Climb on my trunk, swing from my branches, eat my apples, sleep under my shade.' You're our giving tree. You're doing all of this for us."

I was utterly speechless. Dillon, in his innocence, had captured the very essence of my inner struggle, as well as the underlying meaning of Shel Silverstein's book. The giving tree, a symbol of selfless sacrifice, reflected the exhaustion eating away at me. And though I willingly carried it, the weight of it all threatened to crush me.

I held out my hand, and instantly he grabbed it.

"I love you, baby."

"I love you too, Mom."

The following days at Cape Cod unfolded like a magical reprieve from our harsh reality. Jim and Robin were incredible hosts, and the six of us bonded as one big extended family. Together, we enjoyed the serene beaches, playful waves, and long scenic bike rides. The laughter and joy that filled our days momentarily eased the weight of our troubles. But as each night fell, a different energy emerged. And while the boys sought distraction in video games and movies in the basement, I found myself entrenched in emotionally charged conversations with Richard, spending hours on the phone upstairs in Jim and Robin's guest room.

Despite the DC debacle and Richard's insistence on moving out, he began to open up about his doubts. Then on our last night there, he cried and pleaded, "Just come home."

While I was filled with mixed emotions, including a ton of anger, I wasn't ready to give up—not on us, and not on our family. Apparently, neither was Richard.

And so, the roller coaster continued.

Chapter Three
Hello, Me—Welcome Back

One night six months later, in the thick of it all and over a bottle of vino, my best friend, Amy, asked for some advice—a refreshing twist because for months she had been my rock.

While most of my friends had turned their back on me by now, gossiping to each other about my inability to kick Richard's ass to the curb and what they believed was my misguided desire to save my family, Amy never left my side. Together, we would spend hours sitting in the swing that hung from a branch of my front yard's old oak tree. We'd often talk into the wee hours of the night, drinking endless glasses of wine and sometimes even puffing on cigarettes, which was funny since neither one of us smoked. She was the first person I called after I learned of the affair. And she had been my confidant at every dramatic twist and turn. Her support for me and the boys had no limits and showed me the true meaning of friendship.

Amy was unhappy in her marriage, too, but for reasons different than mine. And tonight, it was my turn to be fully present. She and her husband were building a business together and were at odds over next steps. She had an idea around a new product line, but he wanted her to sit back and let him run the company. Her boundless enthusiasm around this new venture was palpable. It was clear she was ready to fly. Yet, she seemingly had to choose between stepping into her power and pleasing her husband for the sake of their marriage.

My advice that night: "Play it small and let him shine." She sat silent. I did, too.

Looking back, it's hard for me to believe I actually said that. But I was living in hell with a marriage on the rocks, scared of the unknown, and paralyzed by fear. My new normal wasn't something I wished upon my worst enemy, let alone my best friend. Perhaps being the "good wife" would help her marriage. Perhaps being a more submissive one would save mine.

I didn't recognize it at the time, but in some ways, I was becoming my mother—her autonomy slowly eroded by decades of my father's dominating behavior. As a teenager, I secretly viewed her as a coward, never understanding why she stayed. Why didn't she believe that she could build a better life for the two for us—emotionally and financially? Why did she allow my father to disgrace her like that? And why did she think it was okay to let me see it? Today, I now understand that the answers to those questions are far more complex than a young girl can comprehend.

Could I ever be that strong and confident again? I thought. *Like the 13-year-old girl who once found enough strength inside her young body to stand up to her abusive father?* I remember one hot summer day in 1984, when the peaceful sound of the chirping birds outside my bedroom window was eclipsed by screams of terror coming from the floor below. I flew down the flight of stairs so fast that I don't think my feet touched a single step. Once I got to the kitchen, I saw nothing but anger in my father's eyes. His face was red, and beads of sweat began to drip down his forehead. Then, just as my mom began to run toward the open sliding glass door, he lunged toward her with a force so great that together they flew through the screen and toppled to the ground.

The chilling sound of her head hitting the pavement filled me with rage. Then adrenaline kicked in, giving me supernatural strength. And with brute force I clenched my fist and pulled my arm back like a sling-shot ready to launch. The moment my fist struck my father's face, blood began to drip from a cut just below his eye. The blow did more than shatter his glasses—it proved that he could never break my spirit.

Twenty-six years later, I was a mere shadow of my former self. I had always vowed to never *ever* let a man take away my power—and yet here I was, walking that path and encouraging my friend to do the same. For many of us, patriarchal myths still permeate our unconscious. Messages resonate throughout society that tell us we can't survive on our own—that we need a man to be complete: physically, emotionally, and financially.

And many of us, when faced with the possibility of divorce, find our-selves feeling like we've failed as women and mothers, regardless of the circumstances. The shame around these feelings of defeat is immense, and they ultimately drive us to bandage the wounds to keep the peace.

I know this because I lived it.

For 14 months, I desperately tried to save my family, believing that in some way I was to blame for Richard's two-and-a-half-year affair and the current state of our marriage. I thought perhaps becoming a picture-perfect wife would put Humpty Dumpty back together again.

Well, it didn't (and thank God). Finally, I'd had enough.

It was now August 2011 and by then, the five of us were living in Coronado, California, a small island just across the bay from San Diego.

Five months earlier Richard had filed for divorce. Shortly thereafter he tore up the papers. Together, we decided San Diego would be our fresh start. My friends and family thought I was nuts, but honestly—divorced or not—I needed a clean slate.

In that moment, California felt like a homecoming. It was the place where our love story began, and I desperately hoped it would be the place where we'd find our happily ever after. Coronado embodied this dream. The salty air, the soothing waves crashing on the sand, and kids' laughter echoing in the streets as they biked freely throughout the island—it all painted a picture of a laid-back life. It was a welcome escape from the stresses of the past year.

I was fully committed to leaving the past behind and rebuilding our marriage. Naturally, I assumed Richard was, too. Why else would he leave Texas—one of the best states in the country for the sole breadwinner (and one of the worst states for a stay-at-home mom) to get divorced with essentially no alimony laws—to move to a state that would force him to pay one-third of his income to me until a judge decided otherwise?

Cole and Drew were thrilled with our decision, although oblivious to the reasons behind the move. They had always loved our sun-soaked vacations along the West Coast and were excited about the opportunity to grow up at the beach. Dillon, on the other hand, wasn't as enthusiastic. Instead, he was filled with skepticism, doubting that the reconciliation would last or that the move would be worth it. And I couldn't blame him. Uprooting three young boys—pulling them away from family and friends—was heart-wrenching. But moving to California felt like my only option. Every corner of our current town held a painful reminder of Richard's affair. Scrutinizing glances and whispers haunted me everywhere I went. I couldn't take another day of it. It was time to leave.

Our first six weeks in Coronado exceeded my expectations—and Dillon's, too. One afternoon as we rode our bikes home from the grocery store, our wire baskets overflowing with food, he surprised me by sharing how grateful he was that I gave Dad one last chance. As much as I tried to shield him from the truth about his dad's indiscretions, I wasn't successful. Richard seemed to be all in, too, prioritizing family time over work, even planning date nights for the two of us to connect and explore our new surroundings together. Finally, things seemed to be back on track.

Until they weren't.

Since the day Richard tore up the divorce papers and up until that night, I had sworn off searching through his phone for any evidence of *her*. But that night something shifted.

Richard reached over and kissed me as I was flipping through TV channels, searching for some mindless programming. Mumbling about being tired, he headed upstairs to our bedroom. Now alone, I stumbled upon *The Real Housewives*. Ironically, amid the designer handbags and petty squabbles, a woman was describing how her husband's affair unfolded through a trail of incriminating texts. My stomach dropped and an uneasy feeling shot down my spine. *Hmm*, I thought, *maybe just one peek. It wouldn't hurt, would it?*

Shamefully I crept up the stairs, walked past our bedroom, and entered Richard's office where his cell phone lay charging on the desk. Ah, relief—there was nothing. Not a single text or email. But I still had my suspicions. What if he'd been clever? So, I moved to the trash folder. And there they were, staring back at me. Endless messages. A sickening collection of suggestive photos and love notes exchanged over the last few weeks.

Rage consumed me.

This wasn't just about me anymore. This was now about the broken trust and shattered world of our three young sons—whom we just displaced. We pulled them away from the only community they had ever known, promising them a better life. But that dream was now gone. The boys and I were about to be forced to create a new life, alone. And they deserved better.

I did, too.

Fueled by fury, I stormed down the hall and threw open our bedroom door. "Get up!" I roared, "How dare you?" My voice cracked with a mix of anger and heartbreak. He lifted his head from the pillow and just stared back at me like a deer in headlights on a dark country road. He didn't say a single word. I tossed the phone on our bed and yelled, "Get out!"

Richard got up, packed a small suitcase, and slid out the front door. He never stepped foot in that house again.

I filed for divorce.

. . .

I read somewhere that the top 10 disempowering emotions are discomfort, fear, pain, anger, overwhelm, disappointment, guilt, self-doubt, frustration, and loneliness. By now, our divorce was almost final, and twenty-four months had passed since the night I learned of the affair. I had felt every single one of those emotions during all 86,400 seconds of each day.

Sixty-three million seconds over the last two years was a lot of freakin' time to waste. I gave that man some of my best years, and I wasn't about to give him a second more—it was time to get busy.

However, I was lost in a question: *What in the hell am I going to do with the rest of my life?* After all, my 13-year role as CMO—chief mommy officer—wasn't going to attract many job offers. I supposed there was some correlation between negotiating multimillion-dollar deals and refereeing fights over LEGO, but it would be a stretch for a prospective boss to see the connection.

Regardless of any spin factor, the facts didn't lie: I was a 41-year-old stay-at-home mom who would now be raising three boys completely alone. Although we had joint custody, Richard and the pink-haired lady had moved to Arizona to start their new life, so caring for the boys would be my sole responsibility. All variables led to the same conclusion, and it wasn't pretty. I began to revert to my early days as a financial analyst, breaking my situation down into if-then statements—like those formulas from an Excel spreadsheet.

IF I find a job, THEN I can pay the legal fees for this divorce.

IF I find a job, THEN I can pay off my debt (which had climbed to five figures since our separation).

IF I find a job, THEN I can enjoy a good bottle of wine again.

IF I find a job, THEN maybe Jimmy Choo and I can reacquaint.

IF I find a man with money, THEN I will live happily ever after.

Wait . . . did I actually think, let alone believe, that a man was the solution? That was the one and only moment that I believed the pink-haired lady and I had something in common. And *that* was my wake-up call.

It was the call to become fully independent again.

I will sign the checks.

I will pay the bills.

I will buy my own shoes and wine.

And I will create the life I want to live.

And while I knew what I *had* to do, I also knew that doing it was going to be my life's greatest challenge.

Part Two
Establish Your Foundation

As I set out to rebuild my life, I turned to books—plenty of them. But each one seemed to miss the mark. They were written by experts who hadn't lived through what I was experiencing. They didn't understand the gut-wrenching pain of losing everything or the emotional and practical hurdles of finding financial security and redesigning a life. Most were filled with well-meaning rules, tips, and strategies, but they failed to inspire or empower me. Instead, they felt dry, generic, and, quite frankly, like they were written for someone else.

So, I decided to create my own plan. What started as my personal road map soon became the foundation of my writing and the curriculum I've since shared with thousands of women around the country. Seeing the impact of my work has been one of the most rewarding experiences of my life. It's also helped me make peace with my past and realize that it has served a valuable purpose—not only in my life but in the lives of others.

What follows are the exact steps I took to rebuild both financially and emotionally. My hope is that this guide will help you forge your own path to financial freedom and a life you love. Whether you're navigating life single, partnered, or married, and whether you're in your 20s or 60s, these strategies are universal. They are designed to help everyone—regardless of their age or circumstances—take control of their financial and emotional well-being.

I recognize that each of you is on your unique journey with different life experiences and varying levels of familiarity with certain financial concepts. To support you along the way, footnotes throughout the book provide key definitions and additional details for extra clarity. If you need further information, don't hesitate to search the internet—it's an action I still rely on often myself! And to further support your learning, I've included a QR code at the end of the book that links to my website, where you'll find a companion workbook, along with additional information and resources.

As you expand your financial literacy, remember this: There is no shame in not knowing—only in not taking action to learn.

Chapter Four

Step One—Explore Your Relationship with Money

*The better you know yourself, the better your
relationships with the rest of the world.*
—Unknown

Suddenly—well, it felt sudden—on August 31, 2012, I was officially single and the head-of-household. I was solely responsible for providing for the boys—especially with child support being so unreliable—and I had no idea how I would do it. But I did know two things. First, I needed to stop thinking about *our* money (and the fact that all that Richard and I built together over the last 19 years had just been slashed in half) and instead start thinking about *my* money. Second, I needed to change my relationship with it.

Throughout our marriage I was never much of a spender. Don't get me wrong, I had no problem with Richard and me buying big-ticket items, like fine art or custom furnishings. But he had to be the one to physically pay for them. Writing a check for more than a few hundred dollars put a knot in my stomach, and swiping my credit card for anything extravagant felt like a betrayal. But now, with every dollar in my accounts under my control, I found it painful to part with any of it. I lived in constant fear that I was *always* one step away from financial ruin—and it was paralyzing. From the moment I filed for divorce, I'd let money control nearly every aspect of my life until one day—shortly after my divorce was finalized—I stopped and asked myself why.

Our behavior with money—whether spending, saving, investing, or avoiding it altogether—is largely shaped by our upbringing. And because, for many of us, money was a taboo topic, we've been left to interpret our experiences and navigate their emotional toll alone—creating a money story that often gives our dollars far too much power.

To rewrite our script, it's important that we each take the time to explore our relationship with money, unpacking the reasons behind the perceptions we have and decisions we've made. We need to start having meaningful conversations about it—not just with others, but with ourselves. Rather than letting money control us, we need to see it as a tool we can use to turn the vision we have for our lives into reality. And to do this we need to take a hard look at where we are today, where we've been, and where we want to go.

Where Are You Today?

The first step to building a healthy relationship with money is to understand where you stand today—including your money mindset. These underlying beliefs and emotions subtly influence your spending habits, saving goals, and overall financial behaviors—all of which shape your money personality.

Your Money Mindset

There are two primary money mindsets: scarcity and abundance. Those who have a scarcity mindset view money as limited and fear losing it all. This might cause them to hold on to every penny, fear risk, and play life small. On the other hand, those who have an abundance mindset see money as something they can create through effort and knowledge, like starting a business or investing wisely. This can lead them to dream big, take calculated risks, and be confident in their decisions. To help determine your money mindset, ask yourself:

* Do you feel empowered to take control of your financial future or like a victim of your circumstance, sinking in quicksand?
* Are you open to stepping outside your comfort zone or do you prefer to play it safe?
* Do you view failure as a learning opportunity or a sign of limitations?
* Do you live life boldly or do you prefer to sit on the bench?

A scarcity mindset breeds self-doubt and restricts you from reaching your full potential, while an abundance mindset allows you to see opportunities and believe in your ability to make things happen. Regardless of where you are today, your money mindset is not set in stone. (Thank God, or I'd still be drinking Two Buck Chuck.) But change starts with self-awareness. By challenging your limiting beliefs and behaviors around money and focusing on what's possible rather than what seems impossible, you can shift toward an abundance mindset and move one step closer to financial freedom and a life you love.

Your Money Personality

While your money mindset represents your attitude toward money, your money personality is how your beliefs play out in your everyday life.

Let's explore six different money personalities. They are not meant to be labels but rather lenses to understand our financial behaviors. And as you review them, keep three things in mind:

1. **These are not rigid categories.** Our relationship with money can evolve over time—life experiences can shape new financial habits.
2. **Growth is always possible.** Recognizing our habits empowers us to make intentional choices and build healthier behaviors.
3. **You may identify with multiple types.** It's common to exhibit traits from more than one financial personality.

The Giver

She has a heart of gold and is known for her generous spirit. Whether it's a friend in need, a worthy cause, or even a stranger down on their luck, the Giver is always there to lend a hand—or a $20 bill. She's a magnet for good vibes, making everyone feel like they belong. Yet sometimes her desire to help others can come at a cost, leading her to overspend or neglect her own financial needs. Sometimes her generosity can even lead to resenting those she helps.

For the Giver, the key is finding balance. With some thoughtful planning and an increased awareness of when she should say no, the Giver can still do her thing without breaking the bank. And when she finds herself in a pinch, it's important for her to remember that there are plenty of ways to fill others' cups—and her own—that don't cost a dime. In fact, sometimes her time and talents can make an even greater impact than her treasures.

The Trailblazer

She doesn't follow the herd—she leads it. With a clear vision and unwavering ambition, the Trailblazer exudes confidence and embraces thoughtful risks. She is a classic type A: driven, focused, and relentless in pursuit of her success. But here is the twist: Her unstoppable drive is often a double-edged sword. While the Trailblazer crushes it at achieving goals and taking charge, her fierce independence can leave her burned out, reluctant to seek help, and so fixated on the next peak to conquer that she misses the beauty of the journey itself.

To create balance, the Trailblazer must intentionally carve out time for hobbies—whether it's reading, hiking, or simply unplugging. And most importantly, she must learn to ask for help. Because while she may be a master at creating wealth, managing it requires a much different skill set. Recognizing her limitations—time constraints, specialized knowledge, or the power of delegation—can be transformative. By leveraging expertise, outsourcing where needed, and strategically focusing her energy, she'll not only reduce stress but achieve far greater financial success.

The Skeptic

Money? Nah, that's for the fat cats and money-grubbers in the Skeptic's mind. This dose of suspicion keeps her comfortable in her financial rut, even though it cripples her financial progress. The Skeptic is stuck between feeling like she doesn't deserve wealth and freaking out over the thought of chasing it. The result? She keeps doing the same things over and over that keep her feeling, well, financially insecure.

Challenging her self-sabotaging thoughts by writing down her positive qualities may help the Skeptic realize that her worth isn't tied to her bank account. She should consider setting achievable goals and celebrating the wins to help build confidence around money matters. Surrounding herself with people who are financially successful but also kind and generous can reshape her perspective on money. Witnessing how wealth can be used for good can dismantle the assumption that it inherently breeds greed.

The High Roller

She lives for the moment! Fancy things excite her, and experiences are her jam. But saving for the future? Well, not so much. Sometimes emotions—or that fabulous sale—win out and lead to impulsive purchases. It's easy for the High Roller to lose track of her spending, which can sometimes lead to a pile of debt. And this constant pursuit of pleasure might leave her feeling a bit empty inside because deep down she knows life is about much more than "stuff."

Exploring how the High Roller copes with her emotions, like boredom or anxiety, can be a key to reducing impulse purchases. Budgeting apps or spending trackers, along with thoughtful discussions about the link between self-worth and material things, can help her build self-awareness around her spending habits. Transitioning to a cash-only system can also be a powerful tool, limiting her ability to rely on credit cards when she is looking to splurge.

The Penny Pincher

The Penny Pincher is a perpetual saver, regardless of how much she has in the bank. She is disciplined and resourceful when it comes to spending (which is a good thing!) and often feels guilty after making a purchase—even when it's a necessity. She is typically debt and risk adverse and has a fear of losing it all, which can cause her to miss out on opportunities to effectively grow her wealth and/or benefit from valuable experiences.

Learning the basics of investing can empower the Penny Pincher to take calculated risks and see the potential benefits that go beyond just saving. Setting specific spending goals, like a dream vacation or fun nights out, can help her shift her focus from what she might lose to what her money can help her gain and experience. This approach can build confidence and create a more balanced financial perspective.

The Avoider

The Avoider believes that, being well off or not, money is a fraught subject and would rather not think about it, let alone talk about it. Money gives her constant agita. Market having a rough patch? She avoids looking at the news for, oh, a year or so. The Avoider generally has no idea where she stands financially. And frankly, she has no idea where to start. Yet the more she avoids pulling her head out of the sand, the greater her anxiety becomes.

Even the smallest actions can ignite change. Whether it's dedicating just 10 minutes each week to reviewing account balances, exploring apps for tracking expenses, or reaching out to a trusted friend for advice, embracing manageable steps can empower the Avoider to confront her financial situation with less stress. Additionally, seeking out resources like online articles, podcasts, or financial literacy classes can help provide actionable steps to improve her financial well-being and build support.

• • •

So, how do you relate to money? Perhaps you recognize parts of yourself in some of these behaviors. As you reflect on your money personality, consider the following:

* Do you struggle to enjoy your money, knowing others have far less?
* Do you turn to retail therapy when you're stressed?
* Does spending money make you anxious?
* Are you ready to take control of your finances but not sure where to start?
* Do you sometimes judge those with wealth, assuming they're entitled or pretentious?

* Have you ever talked about making a big purchase—like a vacation—but rarely follow through because it's hard to pull the trigger and actually spend the money?
* Do you live beyond your means?

Next, take it a step further. Have you ever considered how your money habits impact others—your friends, spouse, partner, or even your children? Remember they each have a money personality, too—and it's likely not the same as yours. This means they may react or interpret financial situations differently than you do.

About six months after my divorce, I began making significant changes. (I will get into the nitty-gritty of all that in the next chapter.) I sold my car and house, downsizing to more affordable options in pursuit of saving to start a business. I even sat through one of those time-share presentations at The Lawrence Welk Resort—enticed by the promise of a free TV.

Then, one evening over dinner—a mishmash of leftovers from the past few nights—Cole looked up and asked, "Mom, are we poor?"

Oops!

I had been so focused on embracing my inner Penny Pincher that I forgot to explain my choices to my kids. Instead of understanding my aspirations for our family, they were left to draw their own conclusions—and they weren't the right ones. That moment was a powerful reminder: Our financial choices don't just affect us—they shape the perceptions, experiences, and behaviors of those around us. It reinforced the importance of open conversations about money, creating opportunities for shared understanding, and inviting our loved ones to be part of the journey, not just bystanders to it.

Where Have You Been?

Your relationship with money didn't just form overnight—it's been shaped by your experiences, your beliefs, and the messages you've absorbed throughout your life. And understanding your past financial influences is key to recognizing why you interact with money the way you do today.

The way you think about money is often rooted in early experiences and lifelong conditioning—these are your money messages. Think of them as seeds planted in your financial mindset, growing into habits and beliefs you carry today. For example, if you grew up hearing "It's not polite to talk about money," you might avoid financial discussion altogether. If you were told "Rich people are greedy," you may associate wealth with negativity. Or if you learned "Investing is a man's job," you might hesitate to take control of your financial future.

But money messages aren't just about what we hear, and they aren't simply about repeating behaviors—they're also shaped by what we see (or don't see) and the actions (or inactions) of those around us. These messages can impact us both positively and negatively, and even the briefest encounter can leave a lasting imprint on our financial mindset—either reinforcing the behavior or pushing us to run in the opposite direction.

Don't misunderstand. There is no single "right" way to view money, but there are likely things you've been unconsciously telling yourself that make life more challenging for you. Building self-awareness around these messages is another step toward creating a healthier relationship with your wealth. For example, I grew up in a sprawling suburban house in a prestigious neighborhood—worlds away from our earlier days in Rockford, Illinois. My parents drove luxury cars, and belonging to an exclusive country club felt like the norm. But that illusion shattered when I learned that my dad—who managed all the money—was forced to immediately sell a car he won after a hole in one in a golf tournament just to pay our taxes that year. Discovering this hidden debt and a lifestyle fueled by credit left me feeling shocked and confused.

That experience instilled in me a deep belief in financial security over spending, prompting me to respond in the exact opposite way of what I had witnessed. The "Money should be saved, not spent" message became a core principle in my approach to money. I never *ever* wanted to experience the level of stress my parents had. Which is why, the day after my divorce was finalized, I took that principal to an extreme, ultimately falling into a scarcity mindset, anxious that I would never achieve financial security again, especially as an unemployed single mother. But if I wanted to take charge of my life, that money story had to change.

Now it's your turn! To understand the root of your relationship with money, consider these questions about your childhood:

1. Who in your family managed the money? Who made the day-to-day decisions and who handled long-term financial planning?
2. Was money a constant source of stress or conflict?
3. Was money ever used as a source of control?
4. Did you ever feel like money was scarce?
5. Was money a topic openly discussed, or was it considered taboo?
6. Were you encouraged to learn about money? If so, how?
7. Did you grow up with any assumptions or judgments about people based on their wealth (or lack thereof)?
8. Can you recall specific memories that significantly impacted your views on money? And what money messages did you take away from those experiences?

Because our past often shapes our present, consider these questions about your current situation:

1. Who in your family manages the money? Who makes the day-to-day decisions, and who handles the long-term financial planning?
2. Do you talk freely about money with your spouse or partner?
3. Does money cause stress for you and/or your family?

4. What money messages exist within your family?
5. How would your kids describe *your* relationship with money?
6. Is money taboo or do you openly talk with your kids about money matters?

By reflecting on your responses to these questions, you can craft your personal money story, revealing hidden roadblocks that might be keeping you stuck. Self-refection isn't about judgment—of ourselves or our parents. It's about empowerment and gaining awareness around what can help propel us forward and, most importantly, what might be holding us back. This introspection is important as we contemplate where we want to go.

Where Do You Want to Go?

Let's face it: Life is a series of twists and turns, and despite our best efforts, many of us wake up one day at a crossroads, realizing the path we're on doesn't spark joy. We just go through the motions each day, handling daily demands, putting our own desires aside, and existing rather than truly living. But often, it's our setbacks—even the moments that leave us breathless, curled up on the floor sobbing—that create a unique opportunity for us to change course and forge a new path toward a more authentic and purpose-driven life. And it all starts with a vision—a mental picture of where we want to go.

For some of us, like me, that vision doesn't come easily. After the devastating loss of my marriage, the very idea of crafting a fulfilling future felt crippling. My self-worth was at an all-time low. The thought of returning to a traditional punch-the-clock job, making a fraction of what I did fresh out of college nearly 20 years earlier, held no appeal at all. It would only solidify my current feelings of failure. I craved something more. I longed to rebuild a career but on *my* terms. While I desperately needed to re-establish my earning power, it had to be in a way that fueled my happiness. But what would that even look like?

Everyone kept telling me that I needed to find my purpose—and all that did was pile on the pressure. What exactly is purpose anyway? It implies some grand, singular destiny that defines our entire existence. And with pictures and videos of joyous people seemingly living their best life all over social media, it's easy to fall into the comparison trap. Maybe creating a vision for the future isn't about *finding* anything. Maybe it's about living with intention—leading a proactive, meaningful life rooted in our core values, the things that bring us joy, and the ways we can contribute to the world (even through simple, everyday actions).

Once I realized this, I had an undeniable awakening: My daily actions were completely out of alignment with who I truly was. I had always loved to create, help others, and live boldly—yet, somehow, my life had drifted far from those values. This realization didn't just apply to that single moment; it forced me to look back at the choices that had shaped my path. I thought back to my early career decisions, when I landed what I believed was my dream job as an investment banker, later moving into private equity.

Was it truly a dream job? Or was it just a socially validated, financially lucrative path I followed without questioning whether it aligned with who I really was?

For years, I had measured success by financial rewards alone. But now, standing at this pivotal moment, I saw an opportunity—a chance to lean in, redefine my future, and forge a new path that would both align with my values and passions and allow me to monetize my purpose, creating a career that felt fulfilling, meaningful, and deeply connected to the life I truly wanted. This wasn't just about work—it was about choosing a life that felt authentic, impactful, and unapologetically mine.

Over five years later, after I had started my businesses, I met a wonderful woman named Maria. She attended one of my financial literacy workshops. I had just introduced a self-assessment tool—a 20-question quiz that categorized general interests into three areas: learning, helping, and community; leading and innovating; and creating and exploring. As the group delved into their results, Maria's eyes welled up as she confessed to feeling utterly lost and trapped. With her permission, I shared her results. And the data spoke volumes: 70 percent of her responses aligned with helping, learning, and community; 20 percent with creating and exploring; and only 10 percent with leading and innovating.

"What are some things that have brought you joy in the past?" I asked gently. Her face lit up as she described a pottery class that she took several years earlier that sparked her creativity and desire to learn. Volunteering at Dress for Success, a nonprofit that empowers women reentering the workforce, also brought her immense satisfaction. Compare that past picture with her current reality. "So, Maria," I began, "tell me about your work and how you typically spend your days and evenings." A heavy sigh escaped her lips as she revealed the truth. Two years prior, she'd taken over the family business after her father's passing. Leading a company of over 50 employees was never her dream. Every day was a fire drill, a relentless cycle of strategy and pressure. The weight of responsibility for her employees felt suffocating.

Leadership accounted for 10 percent of her results, but it accounted for a staggering 90 percent of her day. In other words, the bulk of her time was spent on work that did not align with her core values or did not fuel her passions.

As we talked, the solution seemed to click into place for both of us. Maria leaned forward and asked, "So, should I just leave the business?"

"Absolutely not," I reassured her, "unless that's truly what you want. But there's another option. Here's the key: Carve out some space for yourself. Focus on activities that bring you joy and a sense of renewal. Remember your passion for art? Maybe it's time to revisit that with another class. Perhaps finding new ways to give back to your community would reignite your spark. You could even explore incorporating philanthropy into the company culture, creating a win-win for everyone. The bottom line? Find what puts you back in the flow!"

What does it mean to be in the flow? Imagine you're completely absorbed in something you love doing. Maybe you're painting a picture or writing a book, losing yourself in the swirl of colors or the words filling the page. Or perhaps you're at a yoga class, so focused on integrating breath and movement that you forget about everything else. Maybe you're diving into a research project, piecing together information from various sources, and uncovering new insights when you look up to discover half the day has passed. That feeling of being totally immersed and in the zone—that's what being in the flow is all about.

According to Mihaly Csikszentmihalyi, a leading researcher in positive psychology and the architect of the notion of flow, entering flow is the secret to happiness. Because when you're in the flow, you're completely engrossed and energized by the task at hand. This intense level of engagement suggests a natural alignment with your interests and potential passions.

To me, flow is nothing short of magical, and it can be a powerful tool to uncover what gets you pumped. By paying attention to the activities that trigger flow experiences, you can gain valuable insights into what excites and motivates you, and what you need to lean into as you work to establish a vision for your future.

Now, consider this: Are you currently living a life that you love, or do you need to make some changes?

I'm often asked whether there's anything I've read or heard that's had a profound impact on my thinking that might also help others facing similar circumstances. Without question, it's the spoken words of artist and filmmaker Prince Ea in his video "Everybody Dies, but Not Everybody Lives."[15] During my darkest days, I stumbled upon this powerful video (thank you, Oprah!). It immediately helped me see that, as painful as my journey was, it was actually a gift that created exciting new opportunities. My sadness transformed into profound gratitude. His poetic performance serves as a reminder that every person on this earth has a gift to share with the world. And to maximize our impact, we must deliver that gift with full force, warding off the greatest sabotage: self-doubt. Passion and purpose choose us—not the other way around.

Take a moment to listen to Prince Ea's words (trust me—give yourself this gift) as you explore the following:

* **Have an honest conversation with yourself.** Are you truly passionate about what you're doing today? Does it bring you joy? Are you contributing to something bigger than yourself? Have you thought about the legacy you want to leave in this world? Or are you currently living someone else's dream instead of your own?

* **Stop searching for purpose—chase the feeling.** What makes you feel happy, fulfilled, or (my personal favorite) in the flow? Is there something that feels unfinished—a goal you once set, an interest you once explored, or a dream you pushed aside because life got in the way? Purpose isn't something you find; it's something you feel.

* **Say "Why not?" more often.** Give yourself permission to explore without pressure. Try a new hobby, volunteer somewhere unexpected, take a class that piques your interest, or even plan a spontaneous weekend getaway. Take a chance! You never know what hidden passions you might uncover—or who you might meet along the way.

* **Be kind to yourself.** This is a journey, not a race. It takes time to figure things out. Just start exploring, follow your curiosity, and don't be afraid to take some wrong turns. Maybe you discover a hidden talent for writing or a passion for teaching kids about robotics. The key is to keep moving, keep trying, and stay open—because joy evolves as you grow.

Maybe your vision involves a bold move like starting a business, shifting careers, or traveling the world. Perhaps it's about making small but impactful changes, like prioritizing your well-being or spending more time with loved ones. Whatever the case, once you create a mental picture of where you want to go, commit to it. Set new intentions—this is the first step in turning a hope into something real. Don't be afraid to share your new goals with your friends and family. Change isn't easy, and creating a supportive network of positive people is key to your success. They can help keep you accountable.

You might be wondering what all this has to do with money. A lot! When you're pursuing something you love, something that sparks your passion and brings you joy, you tend to live in an abundance mindset. This opens doors to monetize your passion, build confidence to take risks, and get excited about the possibilities of what you can create.

Now that you have a vision, it's time to take action. Focusing solely on vision without action leads to stagnation. Conversely, acting without clear direction can easily lead us down the wrong path. My life's journey has taught me the importance of balance. No matter how bold your vision is for your future, an equal amount of attention needs to be spent on execution. I firmly believe that when we combine a clear vision with focused action, the possibilities for our next chapter are endless.

So, let's go!

Chapter Five

Step Two—Know Your Numbers

> *Truth is the most valuable thing we*
> *have. Let us economize it.*
> —Mark Twain, *Following the Equator*

By the time my divorce was final, I was saddled with debt. My credit card balance was less than $2,000 the day we separated. Twelve months—and one hell of a contentious split—later, it had grown to nearly $30,000. Sure, I had plenty of airline miles but no money to spend once I got anywhere. I still owed my attorney almost $20,000, and in just two months I had to come up with another $7,000 for property taxes on a house I could not afford. Simple logic told me that since I couldn't control the inflow of money (at least not yet), I had to focus on what I could control. That meant taking a hard look at my numbers—and that should be your next step, too.

The goal of this chapter is to help you:

* Get organized with your money
* Think about your net worth, not just your income
* Understand your ins and your outs
* Put your current spending in perspective

Get Organized with Your Money

The first step to understanding your numbers is to locate where all your money lives. This might sound like an obvious and easy task, and for some people it is. But for others, not so much. Take Judith, for example. When her parents died, she discovered they had over 40 separate accounts with amounts ranging from $20 to around $100,000. Why? Well, there was a time when banks would offer not just high interest rates but things like radios and toasters to entice people to open new accounts. Her father liked toasters. A lot. His attitude about all of this didn't help, either. Shortly before his death, when she was panicked over the chaos of her parents' financial life, his cheerful response was: "Well, that's about to become your problem, isn't it?"

This lack of organization is more common than you might think. The average American holds over five bank accounts.[16] Nearly two-thirds of households also have investments, including retirement accounts like individual retirement accounts (IRAs) or 401(k)s and taxable accounts for stocks, bonds, or mutual funds. Add health savings accounts (HSAs), life insurance, credit cards, auto loans, student loans, and mortgages to the mix, and it's easy to see how our money ends up scattered all over the place.

Getting organized starts with making a comprehensive list of all your accounts. And I don't mean just the financial ones where your money sits—dig deeper! Include any accounts tied to services you use or memberships you hold—literally anything that your money flows into or out of each month. Think insurance providers, cell service carriers, utility companies, private clubs, and gym memberships. Every one of them counts!

Next, get familiar with the details. For each account, document the name of the institution, account number, and whether you currently have online access. For your financial accounts, take a hard look at how each is titled—in other words, whose name(s) is on it. Keep in mind that ownership doesn't guarantee access. Just because you have legal rights to the account doesn't mean you can access the funds if your name isn't on the account. This goes for your debts as well. Even if your name is not on an account with your spouse, you could still be held legally responsible for any outstanding balance. A 2024 Bank Rate study revealed a surprising truth: Nearly a quarter (23 percent) of people are currently keeping some form of secret debt from their spouse or partner, with a secret credit card being a common culprit (17 percent).[17]

A great first step to identifying all your credit accounts—as well as your credit score—is to run your credit report. And once you do, dive into the details of each type of debt, including the interest rate, minimum payment due, length of time you have to pay it back, impact if you pay down a lump sum, and any penalties if you decide to pay it off early.

This exercise was a game changer for me as I worked to tackle my mountain of debt. Sifting through the credit card statements, with their tiny font and baffling legalese, I unearthed a gem: a card with a shockingly low 5 percent annual percentage rate (APR).* Compared to the usurious 18.9 percent on my other card, it was a lifesaver. Staring down two nearly maxed-out cards, my strategy became clear. And I put all the cash I could toward paying down the high-interest card and allocated

---

* Annual percentage rate (APR) is the annualized cost of borrowing money, expressed as a percentage. It includes the interest rate, as well as any fees incurred when you borrowed the money.

just enough to meet the minimum payments to the low-interest card until the other was paid off.

Today, even though both cards have a zero balance, I still manage each card strategically. Because of interest rate hikes in 2022 and 2023, that 5 percent card now sits at 9 percent—still a huge bargain compared to most offers. My other card, despite its whopping 27.24 percent APR (ouch!), boasts an amazing rewards program. And because I always pay it off in full every month, this card is now my go-to for everyday purchases, racking up points instead of interest charges. As for the low-interest card? That one's become my emergency backup, ready in case a financial storm hits and I need a temporary safety net.

Think About Your Net Worth, Not Just Your Income

The dollar amount of our paychecks often becomes a source of fixation, a single number we use to define our overall financial health. But what matters *far* more than our income is what we do with those hard-earned dollars and what we allow those dollars to do for us over time to build our net worth. In fact, often your money can grow faster than you can earn it. But only if you let it!

Your Net Worth = Your Assets – Your Liabilities

By definition, your net worth equals your assets minus your liabilities. Simply put: It's what you own minus what you owe, or as I like to think it's what's left over after you subtract your bad habits from your good ones.

According to a 2024 Payroll.org survey, about 78 percent of Americans live paycheck to paycheck, with little to no emergency fund. They're not only walking a fine line between financial ruin and survival but they're also trapped in a cycle that might keep them working indefinitely, with no clear way out. But it doesn't have to be this way! Building your net worth is essential, and there are *only* four ways to do it:

1. Invest the money you earn.
2. Invest in yourself to help you earn more (and ultimately invest more).
3. Reinvest your profits.
4. Pay down debt—not necessarily all of your debt, just the bad kind (like high-interest credit card debt).

To maximize your money's earning power, start by taking a hard look at everything you own and owe and what those assets and liabilities are currently doing (or not doing) to grow your wealth.

Your Assets

Generally speaking, there are three categories for the things you own: personal property, real property, and financial assets. Personal property includes the stuff you can see, touch, and easily move from one place to another, such as cars, boats, art, jewelry, or other collectibles. Personal property also includes nonphysical assets such as copyrights, royalties, and even club memberships.

Real property is the stuff you own that you can see and touch but that you can't exactly move. Think of it as land and anything permanently stuck to it, like houses, buildings, or even natural resources growing on or beneath the surface. Owning real property comes with some additional perks. If you discover hidden treasures like oil or gold buried beneath the dirt, in most cases, you own those, too.

A financial asset is basically the nonphysical things you own (like a stock or a bond) that hold value because other people want them. And the

Nine Most Common Retirement Accounts

RETIREMENT ASSET	ASSET DESCRIPTION	CONTRIBUTION LIMITS (2025)	WITHDRAWAL RULES
401(k)	Employer-sponsored plan with pre-tax contributions, tax-deferred growth, and potential employer matching	$23,500 $31,000 for 50+ $34,750 for 60–63 (special catch-up)	Penalty for early withdrawal before 59½
Traditional IRA	Individual retirement account with tax-deferred growth; contributions may be deductible	$7,000 $8,000 for 50+	Penalties and taxes before 59½, required minimum distribution at 73
Roth IRA	IRA with after-tax contributions; qualified withdrawals are tax-free	$7,000 $8,000 for 50+	No taxes on qualified withdrawals after 59½
Rollover IRA	IRA used to roll over funds from an employer-sponsored retirement plan	Based on rollover amount	Follows traditional IRA withdrawal rules
SEP IRA	For self-employed or small business owners; tax-deductible contributions; tax-deferred growth	$70,000 or 25% of compensation	Early withdrawal penalties before 59½
SIMPLE IRA	Employer-sponsored IRA allowing both employee and employer contributions, as well as tax-deferred growth	$16,500 $20,000 for 50+ $21,750 for 60–63 (special catch-up)	Early withdrawal penalties before 59½
Roth 401(k)	After-tax contributions with tax-free withdrawals in retirement	$23,500 $31,000 for 50+ $34,750 for 60–63 (special catch-up)	No taxes on qualified withdrawals after age 59½, same contribution limits as traditional 401(k)
457(b)	Deferred compensation plan for state/local government employees and nonprofits	$23,500 $31,000 for 50+	No early withdrawal penalty, but withdrawals taxed as income
Health Savings Account (HSA)	Tax-advantaged savings for medical expenses, with potential retirement benefits	$4,300 individual $8,550 family $1,000 for 55+ (catch-up)	Penalty-free withdrawals for medical expenses, 20% penalty before age 65 for non-medical use

more others want them, the more they are worth. Other financial assets include cash, bank deposits, CDs,* mutual funds,† exchange-traded funds (ETFs),‡ and pension§ or retirement accounts—just to name a few.

When it comes to retirement assets, they are not made equally. Each type of account offers different tax advantages, contribution limits, and rules for withdrawals. The nine most common types are 401(k)s, traditional IRAs, Roth IRAs, rollover IRAs, Simplified Employment Pension (SEP) IRAs, Savings Incentive Match Plan for Employees (SIMPLE) IRAs, Roth 401(k)s, 457(b)s, and HSAs.

Other financial assets are more complex, such as annuities, whole life insurance policies, college savings plans, cryptocurrency, business interests, and private equity. Let me provide some basic definitions:

* **Annuities:** A financial product offered by insurance companies that provides a guaranteed income stream, typically used for retirement planning. You invest money into an annuity, and in return the insurance company pays you a regular income—either for a set period or the rest of your life.

---

* CD stands for certificate of deposit, and CDs are savings accounts offered by banks or credit unions where you agree to leave your money in the account for a set amount of time. In return you earn a fixed interest rate. Typically, you pay a penalty fee if you withdraw the money early. Overall CDs are a safe way to earn more interest than a regular savings account.

† A mutual fund is a pool of money collected from many individuals and invested by a professional manager in a mix of stocks, bonds, and other assets. It's an easy way to invest without having to pick individual stocks yourself.

‡ An exchange-traded fund (ETF) is a basket of investments (like stocks and bonds) that you can buy and sell on the stock market. It's similar to a mutual fund, but ETFs are traded on the exchange all day long rather than just once a day.

§ A pension is a type of retirement plan where your employer sets aside money for you while you work—and then pays you a steady income after you retire.

✳ **Whole life insurance policies:** Type of life insurance that lasts your entire lifetime and includes a built-in savings component. The cash value of the policy is considered an asset. In contrast, term life insurance is not considered an asset since it only provides a death benefit with no savings or investment component.

✳ **College savings plans:** A special type of investment account designed to help families pay for future education expenses, including tuition, housing, books, and other school expenses. The most common type of college savings plan is called a 529 plan.

✳ **Cryptocurrency (crypto):** Digital money that operates on a computer network, allowing people to send and receive payments directly without relying on a bank. Unlike traditional money, crypto is decentralized, which means it's not controlled by a government or financial institution. Instead, transactions are recorded on blockchain—a secure digital ledger that ensures accuracy and prevents fraud.

✳ **Business interests:** Ownership in a privately held business where you own part or all of the company. If you own less than 50 percent, you have a minority interest, and if you own more than 50 percent, you have a majority interest.

✳ **Private equity:** Ownership in a fund that invests in a pool of privately held businesses. Private equity funds typically focus on established companies rather than start-ups, aiming to improve and grow the business before selling for a profit. These funds are generally structured as partnerships.

As you work to better understand what you currently own, it's important you consider the liquidity of each asset—meaning how easily and quickly it can be sold. Typically, if an asset can be converted into cash within a week or less, it's considered liquid. Examples include stocks, bonds, mutual funds, ETFs, and short-term CDs. On the other hand, assets like real estate, private equity interests, and collectables (such as fine art or wine) may take months or even years to sell, so they are considered highly illiquid.

Your Liabilities

Think of liabilities (or debts) as the flip side of assets—they are the financial obligations you owe. These include things like your mortgage, lines of credit, auto loans or leases, student loans, and balances on your credit cards.

Growing up, one of the common money messages you might have heard is "All debt is bad." Well, I'm here to tell you that's simply not true. In a nutshell, "good" debt helps you build your net worth while "bad" debt takes away from it. Examples of good debt typically include a mortgage loan, a business loan, or a student loan. The proceeds from these types of loans are used to invest in assets like a primary residence, an investment property, a business venture, or a person's earning potential. It's all about accessing money at a relatively low cost and putting it to work at a higher rate to help grow your wealth. I'll dive into this in much more detail in the next chapter, but for now, here's a comparison of good debt and bad debt—generally speaking, of course.

"GOOD" DEBT	"BAD" DEBT
🙂	🙁
Mortgage loans	Credit cards
Home equity loans	Auto loans (most of the time)
Student loans	Personal loans
Business loans	Cash advance loans
Auto loans (sometimes)	Layaway loans

Liabilities can also be for things you need to pay for in the future, such as taxes, college tuition, a charitable pledge, or even a commitment you made to help support a family member. And although future obligations might not be part of your current net worth, they can certainly impact your financial health down the road, so it's important you begin to take inventory of them, too.

Your Net Worth

To determine your current net worth, start by listing everything you own along with the current value of each item. Begin with your list of accounts. Then, take the time to identify anything else you have that isn't on that list, likely some personal and real property. Nix the stuff that doesn't have any value. For example, your furniture and worn-out clothing don't count.

Do include valuable personal assets—your home, investment property, car, art, and maybe even a club membership, if all or part of the initiation fee is refundable if you choose to leave. Account for your financial assets, too—your bank, investment, and retirement accounts; other holdings with a cash value, like college saving plans or whole life insurance policies; and anything else you have an ownership interest in.

When assessing the current value of each asset, it is important to understand the difference between cost basis and market value. Cost basis is the original price you paid for something (plus any additional costs like commissions or fees), and as long as you own that asset, that value never changes. It's primarily used to calculate your profit (e.g., your capital gain) or loss on your tax return when you sell the asset. On the other hand, an asset's market value is the price you can sell it for today. In an ideal world (which, as you probably know from the news, doesn't exist), the market value of your assets is substantially higher than their cost basis, meaning their values are consistently increasing. But the reality is that some of your personal assets depreciate—meaning the price you paid is a lot more than what you can sell it for today. Take your car, for example: A brand-new vehicle loses about 9 percent of its value the second you drive it off the lot and roughly 60 percent after five years.[18]

The same valuation principle applies to nearly all your investment- and retirement-related financial assets. Each has a cost basis, which is the original price you paid for that asset. The market value, on the other hand, is what another investor is willing to pay for it today. For assets that can easily be sold, like stocks traded on exchanges (NYSE or NAS-DAQ), the market value is easy to assess. But for illiquid assets, like private equity or ownership in private businesses, determining market value is more complex. And often, professional valuation experts are needed to estimate their worth.

Next, list all your outstanding debts along with their current balances. Include all credit accounts, such as the stuff you just found on your credit report—credit card balances, auto loans, mortgages, and so on. Don't forget to include any medical debt you owe to providers or hospitals. Consider any personal loans from friends or family, as well as upcoming bills or financial obligations due within the next 12 months, such as tax payments or tuition. Now, add up all the outstanding balances on your list and subtract it from the grand total of your assets, and voilà, you have your net worth.

Understand Your Ins and Your Outs

The next step in understanding your current financial reality is to gain a clear picture of the money that is coming in and going out each month.

Your Inflows

For most of us, our primary source of income comes from our paychecks. However, we may also receive income from other sources, such as rental properties, spousal support (i.e., alimony), child support, business income, or distributions from investments. Evaluating the sources of your income, along with their reliability and consistency, will help you assess your current financial health and your ability to confidently cover your spending needs over time.

Your Outflows

For decades when it came to my spending, I had blissfully blurred the line between "wants" and "needs"—until my life was turned upside down and the difference between those two things was thrown into stark relief. To maintain my predivorce lifestyle, I realized I would need to immediately bring home five figures each month. And I didn't need or want that kind of pressure.

Each of us may have a moment like this. You might think you're protected from it; I did, too. But here's the thing: Even if you do avoid a life-changing financial shake-up, you should *always* understand your spending because, until you do, you'll never be financially secure. The reality is that most of us struggle to understand our outflows—with an alarming 56 percent of people admitting they have no idea what they spent last month.[19]

Here's how I learned to do it. I began to examine everything. I needed to figure out what my actual needs were. *What were my critical expenses?* That seemed easy enough: My mortgage was clearly a necessity, as were my property taxes, insurance premiums, car payment, cell phone, and grocery bills. But the task quickly became more complicated because each "need" was also based on my "want" to live a certain lifestyle. So, for the prior 12 months, I took a hard look at my spending, tracking every outflow down to the penny. Using credit card and bank statements and cash receipts, I grouped my expenses into three categories: my unavoidables, my not-so-avoidables, and my avoidables—and these categories can help you, too.

Your unavoidables: These necessary expenses help to keep a roof over your head, stay connected to the world, go from place to place, and protect you and your assets. Most (but certainly not all) are fixed costs, which means they generally stay the same. These outflows are for things like:

* **Housing:** Rent or mortgage payments, property taxes, HOA fees, and maintenance or repairs
* **Utilities:** Electricity, water, trash removal, phone, internet, cable
* **Transportation:** Car payment, car maintenance and repairs, public transportation costs
* **Insurance:** Home or renters, auto, umbrella, and medical, including dental and vision (but don't include if your employer pays these premiums or they are deducted from your paycheck)

Your not-so-unavoidables: These expenses are like a shadow. They follow you everywhere, but you have the power to determine how much influence they have over you. Take gas as an example. While it's a necessity if you own a car, how much you spend depends on your driving habits. Combining errands, carpooling, or eliminating a few road trips can significantly reduce your monthly costs. The same goes for groceries. Sure, we all gotta eat. But that doesn't mean we need to enjoy Kobe beef three nights a week or always buy name-brand products.

Your avoidables: These expenses are 100 percent discretionary—think of facials and manicures, a night out with friends, or the new shoes you just had to have. While you might think they are necessary, they are firmly in the wants category.

As I began to group my expenses, it was easy for me to see that I could nix all my avoidables. So, I homed in on the other two categories. I developed a two-part question and applied it to every single expense:

1. Does this purchase fundamentally make my life better?
2. Is there a cost-effective alternative that provides the same benefit?

My answers led to two key conclusions: Damn, I was wasting a hell of a lot of money! And I had a lot more control over this than I thought.

Needing to put a roof over my head didn't mean it had to cover 3,000 square feet. Same went for my grocery bill, which was out of hand thanks to my organic food and wine habit. Within two months, I traded in the big house (along with its big utility bills and big rooms to furnish and clean) for a more manageable condo a few blocks away. I also replaced my SUV (and its high monthly payments, costly maintenance, and gasoline) for a more affordable and reliable sedan.

I kept going. I ditched my gym membership for a bike. I learned to say no more often to my kids (and, wouldn't you know, they still love me). In total, I cut nearly $3,000 off my monthly nut. This not only eased my anxiety about my immediate income needs but also helped me see how I could use some of this extra money to invest in myself and create new opportunities for my future—like starting a business—which could create income and ultimately grow my net worth.

Are you ready to take action? Don't worry, you don't need to follow in my shoes and make drastic changes overnight. Selling your house tomorrow isn't on the agenda! However, I strongly suggest that you immediately examine the last 12 months of your spending. Why a whole year? It might seem like a lot, but some expenses, like property taxes, insurance, and new car tires, aren't monthly bills. Factoring in these less frequent costs will give you a much clearer picture of your overall spending. This exercise takes time, but it's an investment in your future. The insights you gain will be invaluable as you put the lessons from this book into practice. I suspect it might also help you instantly uncover some small ways (and maybe even a few big ways) to cut out some wasteful spending.

Monthly subscriptions are a great example. According to a recent survey by C+R Research, most Americans think they spend $86 a month on subscriptions services, but the actual amount is over 2.5 times higher: $219.[20] Between music streaming, gaming, newspapers, books, or meal-kit deliveries, it all quickly adds up!

The goal is not to put you on a crash diet or stop you from doing the things you love. Instead, it's about helping you see the dollars you might be unnecessarily throwing out the door. It's all about becoming more intentional with spending, not depriving yourself. My hope is that you'll feel empowered and discover what I did: that you barely miss the old, pricier way of doing things and instead feel amazing about your growing savings.

Looking back over a decade later, I can confidently say my quality of life never took a hit. I still traveled and enjoyed the things I loved. The main takeaway? I simply didn't need as much stuff, or as much money, as I thought to live a truly fulfilling life. With that knowledge, I know I'll be just fine when times get tough again. And that, my friend, is worth more than anything else.

Put Your Current Spending in Perspective

Let's be honest: We're more likely to talk about sex, religion, or politics over dinner with friends than money. Even if one of those friends is a financial expert, asking them personal questions like "How much should my house payment be relative to my income?" or "How much should I be spending each month on my car?" during a ladies' night out would be a social faux pas. So, without a go-to person to ask for guidance, many of us rely on educated guesses, then cross our fingers and hope they keep us out of the red.

Unfortunately for most, those guesses often fall short. A recent study by NerdWallet found that nearly 83 percent of Americans overspend even when they have a budget.[21] And often this leads to a reliance on credit cards to cover the gap, further putting folks in a hole.

It's no surprise, then, that a sperate study by LendingTree found 49 percent of Americans lack an emergency savings cushion to handle an unexpected expense.[22]

Personally, I don't believe in budgets. Too often they encourage a scarcity mindset, leading to feelings of deprivation and resentment, which can then backfire and cause impulsive spending. Missing goals can also lead to shame or guilt, emotions we certainly don't need more of in our lives. And, finally, budgeting typically requires you to track your spending, which can be incredibly cumbersome and unrealistic.

Instead, I prefer a much more empowering tool, like the 45-20-35 model. It's a framework to help you assess your current spending habits, create a target to work toward, and ultimately become more intentional about how you spend your income relative to your current situation and future goals. It's all about understanding your outflows relative to your inflows, which is even more beneficial than only knowing the dollars you spend.

Ideally, *no more* than 45 percent of your monthly after-tax income should be spent on your unavoidables—those essential and reoccurring monthly expenses that, as a reminder, consist of housing and transportation costs, utility bills, and any health insurance premiums that are not already covered by your employer or deducted from your paycheck.

At least 20 percent of that monthly income should be consistently invested in your future to help build your net worth. This is beyond any pretax contributions you make to an employee retirement plan, such as a 401(k) or 403(b), and it should be considered a non-negotiable expense. Depending on your circumstance, these funds might be used to:

* Grow your emergency fund to cover six to nine months' worth of living expenses
* Pay down bad debt (see chapter 6)
* Maximize contributions to non-employer-sponsored retirement accounts, like a traditional or Roth IRA

Your 45-20-35 Model

No More Than 45%

of your net monthly income should be spent on UNAVOIDABLES.

30%	5%	5%	5%
HOUSING	TRANSPORTATION	UTILITIES	INSURANCE

At Least 20%

of your net monthly income should be put toward your future!

- Grow emergency fund
- Pay down bad debt
- Add to retirement accounts
- Invest in other assets
- Invest in yourself

Make it non-negotiable and use it to grow your net worth.
How you apply it depends on your situation and goals!

What About the Remaining 35%?

This is your empowerment money.
It's money that you can take charge of!

- Consists of needs (not-so-avoidable) and wants (avoidables); both of which are variable
- Fluctuates by the decisions YOU make

* Save to invest in other assets (e.g., taxable investment accounts or investment properties)
* Invest in *yourself*—a professional accreditation, a writing class, or even taking a page out of Bobbi Brown's playbook and signing up for hip-hop dance lessons

The remaining 35 percent is what I call empowerment money and should be put toward your not-so-avoidable and avoidable expenses, covering things like food, entertainment, clothing, and vacations. This is the money you can take charge of. And by making smart choices about these expenses, you can free up more money for the things you enjoy or simply might need.

In other words, let's say the cost of living is extraordinarily high where you live, and you need to subsidize your monthly unavoidables (or essential expenses). No problem, you'll just need to reduce the amount you put toward your empowerment money to make up the difference.

And if you don't? Well, that's where most people get into trouble. Instead of proactively making smart choices to reduce their avoidable (i.e., discretionary) spending or finding ways to save on their not-so-avoidables (e.g., burgers instead of steaks, outlet stores over designer brands, or carpooling to cut gas costs), they turn to their savings—or, worse, their high-interest credit cards—to fund the difference. And both can take a serious toll on your net worth.

Take Holly, for example, a recent divorcée with two kids, Jake (18) and Will (14). Her total monthly after-tax income, which includes child support for Will and wages from her job as a dental hygienist, is $5,420.

Under the 45-20-35 model, Holly should aim to spend no more than $2,440 on her unavoidables and invest at least $1,080 in her future, leaving almost $1900 a month for her not-so-avoidables and avoidables. However, she is currently spending:

* $2,550 (47 percent of her inflows) on her essential monthly expenses (not bad!)
* $500 (9 percent of her inflows) to pay down the $2,500 balance on one of her credit cards
* $2,600 (48 percent of her inflows) on everything else

By looking at her spending this way, she can quickly see that her total spending ($5,650) exceeds 100 percent, indicating that Holly is overspending by 4 percent, which is the likely cause of her growing credit card balance.

Although Holly might find ways to shave a few extra dollars off her monthly unavoidables to bring that percentage down to 45, what's even more critical is for her to start saying no to more of her monthly wants. This will allow her to increase her savings by at least $580 a month—first putting it toward her emergency fund so she can become less reliant on her credit cards for those unexpected but necessary expenses. Once the outstanding balance on her credit card is paid off, Holly can explore other investment opportunities for the $500 previously allocated to debt repayment.

Now it's your turn! In chapter 7, we'll be diving deeper into all of this and explore how to incorporate it into your overall financial plan. To get the most out of that section, it's important to first understand how your current monthly spending compares to your total monthly income. And don't worry if your spending doesn't align with the 45-20-35 model just yet—I'll share practical strategies to help you get there.

Chapter Six

Step Three—Expand
Your Knowledge

Knowledge is power.
—Sir Francis Bacon

Pay cash for everything."

"All debt is bad."

"Buying over renting is always best."

"Pay off all credit card debt before you do anything else."

These are just a few examples of financial advice you might hear from leading experts. But beware! Before you act on any of it, you should know that even the "best" financial advice might not be what's best for you. Each one of us is unique, with different earning powers, desires, priorities, goals, and available resources. You should consider these factors and more, such as your age or stage in life, when making any financial decisions. My advice to a 30-something on the best way to finance a home would likely differ from what I'd recommend to a woman in her 60s. For example, as you approach your golden years, minimizing your monthly expenses becomes increasingly important—especially when you decide to stop working and start relying on your nest egg to meet your monthly lifestyle needs. Therefore, using a significant amount of cash to minimize—perhaps even eliminate—the amount you need to borrow might be wise. On the other hand, one of the greatest assets a young person has is their earning power, which gives them the flexibility to potentially take on a larger mortgage and invest in a property that can appreciate over time.

The fact is, taking any advice at face value, or blindly following a rule or formula, doesn't do anything to increase your financial know-how or help you make confident decisions. Instead, it's important that you equip yourself with tools that empower your decision-making process. Long-term success will happen only when you learn the *why* behind the advice and then decide for yourself whether to take it or leave it! And it all starts with a comprehensive understanding of the four financial principles that unlock your money's full potential and, consequently, your overall financial well-being:

* Opportunity cost
* Compounding
* Arbitrage
* Diversification

While on the surface these terms might seem like highly technical jargon, understanding each concept—and how to apply it to your everyday decision-making—can have a profound impact on your wealth, both now and in the future. In fact, embracing these principles radically changed my life. The day my divorce was final, I had just enough in liquid assets to start over but certainly nowhere near enough to maintain my current lifestyle. Jobless and facing a new reality, I knew I had to put whatever money I had left to work for me—immediately.

At the time, investing felt like running a marathon with absolutely zero training. I didn't know what stocks to pick, how best to fold bonds into the mix, what an ETF was, how to buy a mutual fund, or even the going rate for a 30-year mortgage. Yet I did have a secret weapon: a different kind of financial knowledge. For nearly 20 years, I left all my financial decisions to Richard, so my personal finance experience was zilch. But thanks to my studies at USC, along with my prior career investing in private businesses and helping companies raise capital, my understanding of corporate finance was pretty darn extensive. What if I started to look at *myself* as a business? What if I took everything I learned back then, shifted my thinking, and instead of simply homing in on where to invest my money, I channeled my inner CFO and started to run my financial life the way I'd manage the financial aspect of a business? This thinking was a game changer. I began to see those four key principles in a completely new light, recognizing their simplicity, hidden power, and the impact they could have on my ability to make better financial decisions and grow my wealth—and the ability of others to do the same.

Now, I invite you to adopt this mindset, too. Keep in mind, my goal isn't to teach you where or how to invest—I believe most people should avoid investing on their own. Instead, I hope that by embracing this approach, you'll be more empowered to make informed decisions about managing your money in everyday life. While you may not have the same understanding of these concepts as I did when I started, that's exactly why I am here. In this chapter, I'll explain what these principles mean and give concrete examples of how to use them as tools in your financial decision-making process. Our first stop? Opportunity cost.

Opportunity Cost

As a newly single mom, my auto-response to just about every question that flew out of the mouths of my three sons was yes.

Yes, I will be your room mom!

Yes, I will be the team mom!

Yes, we can still go on vacations, live in our supersize house, drive our big SUV, and eat out several times a week.

And the one that had me really questioning my sanity: *Sure, no problem! I am more than happy to drive six hours round trip to Six Flags Magic Mountain not once but twice over back-to-back weekends, all to spend $500 to stand in long lines in 95-degree heat to ride a roller coaster that will probably make me vomit.*

Like other moms in my shoes, I was haunted by divorce guilt. And as a result, I did everything I could to try to reduce the collateral damage to my boys. Yet, despite my best intentions, all those yeses came at a hefty price. Not only did my face gain a half a dozen more stress-induced wrinkles, but I also became the not-so-proud owner of a big fat credit card balance. And neither was how I wanted to kick off my new life as a single mom. I found myself stewing over this question: What could I have done with all that money if I had simply said no? The answer: *a lot*.

In fact, the longer I stared at my year-end credit card statement, the more I realized the power that lives in that simple two-letter word. Once I began to embrace the idea that a no to one thing can mean a yes to something else (like zero debt, a growing emergency fund, or an expanding investment account), the results were life-changing.

And that, my friend, is opportunity cost.

Technically, opportunity cost is the benefit (or value) that is given up when we chose one thing over another. For example, when a company decides to invest in one project, it gives up the opportunity to invest in another, forgoing the potential benefit that would have been gained from the alternative option. When applied to individuals, opportunity cost is all about the trade-offs inherent in our short-term and long-term decisions. Saying yes to something *always* means saying no to something else.

This principle doesn't just apply to money; opportunity cost also shows up in the constant demands on our time and talents—the pressure we feel to say yes even as we drive ourselves into insanity and exhaustion. Yet, we rarely ever stop to consider the true cost of our decisions—on both our financial and emotional well-being—*before* we make them. And while we can't quantify the cost of all of our yeses, when it comes to our financial ones, it might be easier to do than you think.

Imagine you start saying no to a few tempting wants—an extra shopping trip to Target, a night or two out with friends, or even a daily fancy coffee habit—and start saying yes to saving an extra $100 a month.

Now let's assume you invest that extra $100 each month. Depending on your situation, you might work with your financial advisor—or open a brokerage account on an online platform—and invest in an index fund.* Assuming an average return of 7 percent, after 15 years, you'd have an impressive $31,700—$18,000 of which you personally saved ($100 per month for 15 years), plus another $13,700 that your savings earned for you, without you doing a thing.

How? It's the result of an amazing phenomenon called *compounding*.

Now it's your turn! Are you unintentionally sabotaging your money's ability to work for you? Take a close look at the "avoidables" and "not-so-avoidables" you identified in the last chapter.

Make note of three significant "wants" that you said *yes* to—whether for yourself or your children.

Now, add up the total amount spent on those three purchases. Take a moment to consider the opportunity cost—how that money could have been used to grow your net worth instead.

---

* An index fund is type of mutual fund or exchange-traded fund (ETF) that tries to replicate a specific market index's performance, such as the S&P 500, NASDAQ 100, or Dow Jones Industrial Average. These funds invest in the same securities as the index in the same proportion. The primary objective of an index fund is to match the index's performance as much as possible.

Opportunity Cost = Total Spent + Potential Growth if Invested

FORMULA: Opportunity Cost = Dollar Spent + Dollar Spent x $(1.07)^{20}$

ASSUMES: 20 years at 7% rate return

Finally, take a moment to reflect:

⁎ What, if anything, surprised you about your result?

⁎ If you had known this number ahead of time, would it have influenced your decision to make those purchases? Why or why not?

⁎ Does this new awareness spark any other thoughts or questions for you to explore?

Compounding

Think of compounding as a snowball rolling down a snow-covered hill. While it might start out small, the more it rolls, the more snow it picks up, until suddenly that tiny little ball becomes a huge mass of snow. That's exactly what can happen to your investments over time. Compounding is money earned on the initial dollar amount you invest *plus* the accumulated money you've earned from past periods. It's all about earning interest on interest.

Imagine you invested $1,000, earning 10 percent interest. Each year, you earn interest on the initial $1,000 as well as interest on what you've accumulated. This interest on interest is just like the snowball rolling downhill—it gets bigger and faster over time. In fact, over 30 years that single $1,000 could grow to nearly $18,000!

COMPOUNDING *in Action*

Year 1 .... $1,000 x 10% = $1,100
Year 2 .... $1,100 x 10% = $1,210
Year 3 .... $1,210 x 10% = $1,332
Year 4 .... $1,332 x 10% = $1,464
Year 5 .... $1,464 x 10% = $1,610

At year 30 .... **$17,450**

Compounding is the secret to financial freedom. Because if you do your part, your money will work harder for you than you ever imagined. In fact, for many of us, the money we invest can grow more over time than what we earn from our jobs.

For example, let's assume a 25-year-old opens a traditional IRA and consistently contributes $100 per month, year after year, until retiring at 65. Over 40 years those monthly contributions would add up to $48,000. Not too shabby. But thanks to the power of compounding, and assuming an average return of 7 percent, the actual balance in her IRA account would grow to just over $260,000! Beautiful, eh? Sure, that 25-year-old worked hard for that $48,000, but not nearly as hard as that same $48,000 worked for her—generating almost four and half times more money than the actual dollars she saved.

Now let's supersize it! Imagine the impact of cutting out two, three, or four wants per month—perhaps even saving enough to invest the maximum annual IRA contribution allowed by the IRS in 2025: $19 per day, $583 per month, or $7,000 annually. (And by the way, when you turn 50, that $7,000 increases to $8,000.) Using that same annual return rate, her new balance in that same IRA account could amount to as much as $1,530,000 by the age of 65. Yet, the total dollar amount that she personally saved was only $280,000.

That is powerful!

Obviously, not everyone is 25, with the luxury of time on their side. But don't underestimate the time you do have. With the average woman's life expectancy at 82 years, there is still a lot of muscle left in your dollar. Let's take that previous example but now assume you're 50 and contributing the maximum $667 per month. By the age of 72, you could have an impressive $416,000! So, there is no time like the present to ensure you are maximizing your money's ability to work for you. However, doing so requires the right approach, which means starting now, saving consistently, and investing wisely—because not all assets are created equal.

For example, your home is very different from the investments that make up your retirement account or the cash that's sitting in savings. Each type of asset has different risk and marketability (i.e., the ability to be sold), and both help make up the asset's potential earning power. Typically, the higher the risk, the higher the potential return. We don't have a crystal ball to predict with certainty how each type of asset will grow, but using their historical returns is an effective way to estimate future performance. This is the best way to compare one investment opportunity to another.

Let's look at reasonable expected returns for six different types of assets that typically make up a person's balance sheet: cash, personal property, savings accounts, taxable investment accounts, retirement accounts, and residential property.

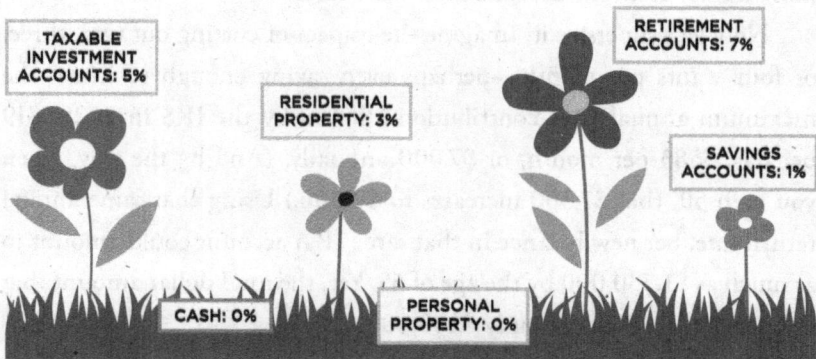

TAXABLE INVESTMENT ACCOUNTS: 5%
RETIREMENT ACCOUNTS: 7%
RESIDENTIAL PROPERTY: 3%
SAVINGS ACCOUNTS: 1%
CASH: 0%
PERSONAL PROPERTY: 0%

For your retirement accounts, it's reasonable to assume an average return of around 7 percent after inflation. Why? The S&P 500 index fund* is commonly used as a benchmark for long-term growth in these types of accounts. Over the past 30 years, this index has historically delivered an average return of about 11 percent annually, or just over 7 percent after inflation. Remember, these assets are meant to grow over the long haul, so it's essential to avoid taking money out of those accounts early. In fact, doing this can lead to serious taxes and penalties—we're talking about a hit of over 50 percent in some cases. Ouch!

Your nonretirement (or taxable) investments, such as brokerage or individual accounts, offer much more flexibility because you can access your money at any time. Because of this, they are viewed as shorter-term investments, so you should expect a lower rate of return—around 5 percent. This is due to having less time to recover from market dips while your money is invested.

When it comes to residential real estate, a safe bet it is to expect a 3 percent annual return. Even though home prices have increased significantly from 2019 to 2024, it's important to remember that expected returns are based on the big picture. Getting caught up in short-term trends can lead to unrealistic goals and poor investment decisions.

As for your savings accounts, that cash under your mattress, or your personal belongings, it's best to assume that you'll make nothing off them. And that vast Beanie Babies collection? While adorable, it's not going to help anyone retire early!

---

* A collection of 500 of the largest publicly traded companies in the United States. It was introduced in the late 1950s and includes institutions like Apple, Microsoft, and Amazon.

Arbitrage

Arbitrage might sound like a fancy word reserved for MBAs or Wall Street, but it's actually a powerful and accessible tool in personal finance. Essentially, arbitrage is the opportunity to profit from the cost difference between two things that resemble one another. It's all about having a keen eye for market inefficiencies and acting on them quickly.

Let's say you go to Italy and discover a beautiful leather bag for half the price you could get a similar bag for in the United States. You buy 20. Then you bring them back with you (disclosing to customs, of course) and sell them to your friends for a higher price than you paid. You pocket the difference between what you paid and what you sold them for. And there you have it: arbitrage. But my guess is you don't plan to become an international handbag merchant, so let me apply the concept of arbitrage to your everyday life.

Rent or own? It's a question many of us grapple with, especially as we pursue the "American dream" while navigating rising housing costs and interest rates. Although we're often told that owning is always the better option, in certain conditions—low rent compared to high investment returns—you might actually be better off leasing and investing the money you save by not buying. But like most financial decisions, to determine this requires you to dive into the details.

Suppose you are looking to buy a house that costs $419,000, which was the median home price in 2024 in the United States, according to the U.S. Department of Housing and Urban Development.[23] You plan to live in it for five years, put down 20 percent ($83,000), and borrow the remaining $335,000 at an interest rate of 6.25 percent. All in, your monthly home expenses—which includes a mortgage payment, taxes, and insurance—would be about $3,400. Now let's assume a similar house down the street just became available to lease for $1,800 per month. The next page examines the overall financial benefit of one option over the other.

Option One – Rent Instead of Buy

ASSUMPTIONS

- You plan to rent the house for $1,800 per month for at least five years
- You invest the $1,600 per month savings from renting (monthly cost of $1,800) instead of buying (monthy cost of $3,400)
- You invest the $83,000 instead of using it as a down payment
- Your investments earn a 7 percent annual return

RESULTS

- The $83,000 and the $1,600 monthly savings grows to $232,000
- Total rent paid over five years is $108,000 ($1,800 per month)
- Your net financial gain from renting is $124,000 ($232,000 – $108,000)

Option Two – Buy Instead of Rent

ASSUMPTIONS

- You buy and live in the house for $3,400 per month for at least five years
- The home value appreciates by 3 percent a year

RESULTS

- Your home will be worth approximately $487,000 after five years
- You have $172,000 of equity (the value of your home minus the outstanding mortgage balance)
- Total mortgage, taxes, and insurance cost you $204,000
- When you sell, you'll pay roughly 6 percent of the sales price in transaction costs, which is nearly $30,000
- Due to mortgage interest and property tax deductions, homeownership provides an estimated $22,000 in tax savings over five years, assuming an 18 percent marginal tax rate.
- Your net loss from owning is $40,000

The Math Behind the Net Loss of Owning

Equity – Homeownership Costs – Transaction Costs + Tax Savings = Net Loss

$172,000 – $204,000 – $30,000 + $22,000 = -$40,000

Conclusion: Is Renting or Owning the Better Choice?

Renting wins decisively in this scenario, providing a $164,000 greater financial benefit over five years compared to buying.

Let's explore another example: buying a car. Should you pay cash or finance it? One money expert says, "You should always pay cash." And in the majority of cases I agree, but not *always*. From the end of 2008 until March of 2022, we were living in one of the lowest interest rate environments ever. Financing a car essentially meant borrowing money for next to nothing. During that same period, the S&P 500's average rate of return was around 12 percent. So, assuming you had the cash readily available, it didn't make much sense to spend it on a depreciating asset (like a car, boat, or RV) when you could borrow at 1 to 2 percent and invest your cash at 12 percent—earning a spread of around 10 percent. After all, either way you buy the car, that asset is going to depreciate. Again, this is arbitrage.

But before you "interest rate arbitrage," it's important to remember that just like assets, not all debt is the same. And whether you should take on new debt comes down to its interest rate, how you plan to use the money you borrow, and of course whether you can afford it. If all three of those boxes get checked, leverage* can help you preserve cash and put an otherwise illiquid asset to work to build your net worth. Let's revisit the concept of "good" debt versus "bad" debt.

"GOOD" DEBT	"BAD" DEBT
🙂	☹️
Mortgage loans	Credit cards
Home equity loans	Auto loans *(most of the time)*
Student loans	Personal loans
Business loans	Cash advance loans
Auto loans *(sometimes)*	Layaway loans

---

* Leverage is the strategic use of borrowed funds to increase potential returns.

As I shared in chapter 5, good debt helps you build your net worth, while bad debt takes away from it. Just a quick reminder, examples of good debt typically include a mortgage loan, a business loan, or a student loan. Proceeds from these types of loans are used to invest in assets like a primary residence, an investment property, a business venture, or a person's earning power. Again, it's all about accessing money at a relatively low cost and putting it to work at a higher rate to help grow your wealth.

Sometimes recognizing good debt from bad debt is easy. But sometimes, not so much. Whether you are evaluating an arbitrage opportunity or not, *anytime* you're considering taking on new debt, ask yourself the following questions—what I call the "good" debt "bad" debt test:

1. **What is the interest rate?** If it's 5 percent or less, it could be good debt. But if it's 8 percent or higher, it's likely not. Why? Because the higher the interest rate, the harder it is to get ahead—what you gain from borrowing is likely far less than what it costs you to carry the debt.

2. **What do you plan to do with the money?** If you plan to put the money toward an appreciating asset—an investment account, a new business, a rental property, or education— it very well could be good debt. But if your plan is to buy a depreciating asset—new clothes, a vacation, some furniture, or possibly even a car—no matter what the interest rate is, that's not-so-good debt.

My goal here is not to encourage you to take on a bunch of loans you don't need to or can't afford. Nor is it to convince you to run out and invest in something you are not completely comfortable with. Instead, I want to encourage you to start looking at money differently, empowering you to see it as tool for creating opportunities and making more informed decisions.

Diversification

It's important to understand that when it comes to your money, you can have too much of a good thing—or not enough of another. To ensure you're maximizing your money's ability to work for you and minimizing your overall risk, you need to have the proper mix of assets. Diversification is the process of not putting all your eggs in one basket. And when it comes to your wealth, it's all about hedging your bets.

Ever heard of Tulip Mania? In the mid-1600s the tulip bulb became so popular in the Dutch Republic that prices soared and a frenzy started. Everyone, from the elite to the common folk, scrambled to invest in tulips—and many of them risked their entire life's savings. In fact, at the peak, rare tulip bulbs were selling for the equivalent of a luxury house or a year's earned income. Well, it wasn't long before the tulip bubble burst, causing many people to lose everything since they put nearly all of their money into a single investment.

Diversification is critical to your overall financial (and mental) health. And not just with speculative investments like tulips. Having too much cash sitting in a savings account can be risky, too. Why? Because of the opportunity cost of not putting enough of that cash to greater use.

Don't get me wrong: As I shared earlier, having enough cash to cover at least six to nine months of expenses (i.e., your emergency fund) is essential because it's important that you're prepared to ride out an unexpected event like a job loss, a medical crisis, an economic downturn, or even a massive car or home repair. But outside of this necessary savings account, studies show that women tend to hold a disproportionate amount of their investable assets in cash, causing them to jeopardize their long-term financial well-being. Remember: Cash doesn't generate investment returns, and it loses value over time thanks to inflation.

To help illustrate the cost of having too much cash, imagine you have a goal to save $300,000 over the next 15 years. Investing in an asset with an annual return of 5 percent would require you to save about $14,000 annually. On the other hand, if you relied on a traditional savings account and earned 1 percent, you'd need to save almost $18,700 each year to reach your goal. Thus, the opportunity cost of investing at 1 percent rather than 5 percent adds up to a sobering $70,500. And that's a lot of earning power you can't afford to waste. Factor in inflation (i.e., how much that $300,000 will buy in the future)—which has averaged around 3 percent historically but peaked at 9 percent in 2022—and ensuring you're maximizing your money's earning power becomes even more critical.

But even if your money is invested in well-preforming assets, a lack of diversification can create another type of risk. Take Jackie's situation as an example. She owns three rental units in Miami in addition to her primary residence. Given the city's post-pandemic economic boom and population growth, these investments are exceeding her expectations, generating some great rental income and property value appreciation. But she still isn't diversified. Even though her properties are scattered throughout the city, if a hurricane hits and causes widespread property damage and a hit to the local economy, all of Jackie's real estate investments—which represents a significant portion of her wealth—could be obliterated. However, if she diversifies her real estate investments into markets outside of Miami, her portfolio would be far less vulnerable. For example, she could purchase a property in Denver and another in Nashville. Even better, from a diversification standpoint, she could keep the residential property in Miami while investing in a commercial property in Denver and invest the remaining funds in a brokerage account. In the event of a hurricane devastating the Miami property, the other two investments could help offset her losses.

That's the power of diversification!

The principle of diversification can be just as important for your income—especially as you age—so you're not entirely dependent on the money you actively earn if it suddenly stops. Sure, having a side gig can help you generate multiple sources of income, but in some cases, so can your investments.

For example, I own investment property—a rental property I purchased just a few years ago. Currently, I reinvest my net monthly rental income.* However, in the years to come, as my career winds down, the profits from the rent I charge will help supplement my retirement funds.

This type of income is called passive income†—often referred to as "mailbox money"—because you invest time or money up front and then collect a reward each month with little to no ongoing effort. It also can help provide some nice diversification.

So how much of your income should be diversified? Well, it depends on your circumstances, tax situation, and goals, which is why you need to make a plan. Here's mine right now: I'm 54 with a steady paycheck and decent amount of investable assets, so only a small amount of my total income is passive. Barring some unforeseen financial emergency, all my passive income is strategically reinvested. But here's where it gets interesting: Once you begin generating passive income, you can invest it in ways that build more wealth and eventually create, yup, even more passive income.

Let's say you net $2,000 of income each month from a piece of rental property. Reinvest that income, like me, and on average earn 7 percent annually. After 10 years, you've got $346,000. In fact, even $500 of additional income each month could turn into almost $90,000 in 10 years, depending on how you invest it. In addition to saving more and

---

* Net monthly rental income is the total rent received minus all operating expenses associated with maintaining the property.

† Passive income is money you earn with little to no ongoing effort after the initial work or investment is made. It typically comes from sources like rental properties, dividends from stocks, or royalties.

putting more money to work, multiple income sources can preserve your net worth. If your main source of income dries up, another source can help minimize the impact until you can replace that income.

Now it's your turn! Are you diversified? First, reflect on the work you did in chapter 5 to better understand what you own and what you owe, then complete the following exercise.

Total Amount of Each Asset Type

REAL PROPERTY

Real Estate	$_____
Minus: Mortgages	$_____
Minus: HELOC	$_____
Total	$_____

INVESTIBLE ASSETS

Investment Accounts	$_____
Retirement Accounts	$_____
Whole Life Insurance (Cash Value)	$_____
Total	$_____

BANK ASSETS

Checking Accounts	$_____
Savings Accounts	$_____
Cash (Safety Deposit Box)	$_____
Total	$_____

OTHER ASSETS

Private Business Interests	$_____
Private Partnerships	$_____
Other Assets	$_____
Total	$_____

TOTAL ASSETS $_____

Type of Asset as a Percentage of Your Total Assets

Real Property	_____%	Investable Assets	_____%
Bank Assets	_____%	Other Assets	_____%

FORMULA: (Type of Asset) ÷ (Your Total Assets) x 100

Now, take a look at your income and proceed with the following steps.

Type of Income (Net of Taxes)		
Salary 1	$_____	Investment Income $_____
Salary 2	$_____	Other 1 $_____
Bonuses/Commissions	$_____	Other 2 $_____
Pension	$_____	Other 3 $_____
Rental Income	$_____	Other 4 $_____
TOTAL NET INCOME $_____		

Type of Income as a Percentage of Your Total Net Income

Salary 1	_____%	Investment Income	_____%
Salary 2	_____%	Other 1	_____%
Bonuses/Commissions	_____%	Other 2	_____%
Pension	_____%	Other 3	_____%
Rental Income	_____%	Other 4	_____%

FORMULA: (Type of Income) ÷ (Your Total Net Income) x 100

Your responses (and more) will be essential as we work to create your personal financial road map in the next chapter.

Part Three

Turn Your Knowledge into Action

Chapter Seven

Step Four—Create a Plan

Action without direction is like
motion without reason.
—Unknown

A lovely woman I recently met confessed that she felt completely overwhelmed by her finances. No matter how hard she worked, she couldn't seem to get ahead—her spending felt out of control, her credit card balance kept growing, and the interest charges swallowed up any attempt she made to pay it down, making it nearly impossible to focus on anything else.

She isn't alone. With some banks charging as much as 36 percent interest on credit card balances, it's easy for debt to quickly spiral out of control. Imagine owing $25,000—if you're only making the minimum payment, it could take nearly 39 years to pay off the balance, costing close to $75,000 in interest alone. That's real money that could be put to better use—helping you buy a home, invest for the future, or build a secure retirement. Yet, this is exactly the kind of financial trap that smart, responsible people fall into.

The problem? Financial security isn't about tackling one issue at a time. It's about stepping back, seeing the bigger picture, and creating a comprehensive plan that aligns with all your financial goals. Without a plan, it's easy to stay stuck in a cycle of reacting to financial problems instead of proactively building wealth and stability. Think about weight loss. You can hit the gym religiously, but if your diet, sleep, and stress levels are out of balance, you won't see lasting results. Sustainable progress requires a holistic approach—nutrition, movement, rest, and stress management all working together. The same principle applies to financial planning. A true, lasting solution requires more than just cutting expenses or paying off one debt at a time. It starts with a clear vision of what you want, an honest assessment of where you stand today, and a thoughtful plan to bridge the gap between the two.

Yet studies reveal that nearly 75 percent of women lack a structured financial plan to guide them toward their goals.[24] And that, my friend, is what we're about to change. In this chapter, you'll learn how to:

* Understand your reality
* Know your vision
* Think 45-20-35
* Be intentional with your assets
* Establish your action steps

And then, you can execute your plan and celebrate the results.

Understand Your Reality

In chapter 5 you surveyed your financial landscape, taking inventory and documenting what you own and what you owe, as well as your monthly inflows and outflow. Now let's dive deeper into what those numbers reveal about your current financial health and your best next steps toward financial freedom. Consider all that you've learned thus far and ask yourself:

* Do I have access to enough cash to weather a financial storm, covering at least six months' worth of my monthly expenses? If not, how much more do I need to save to reach that goal?
* Do I have bad debt to pay off? How much and at what interest rate?
* What good debt do I currently have? How much more of it can I access in case I need it in the future?
* Does my household have one or multiple sources of income? How consistent are my monthly inflows?
* Am I relying on any of my assets to cover a portion of my monthly expenses?
* What's my income potential? What are the things I can do now that will help me earn more in the future?
* How diversified are my assets—very, somewhat, or not at all?
* How liquid are my assets? What can quickly be sold and turned into cash if I need it? What percentage of my money is tied up in my house, a business, or something else that makes it difficult to access? Do I need to mix things up?
* Do I know how much in total assets I'll need to ensure I don't run out of money as I age?

On that last point: I recommend planning that you'll live to 100. A 2024 BlackRock Read on Retirement™ survey found that 65 percent of women today worry about outliving their money. Honestly, this has always been one of my biggest concerns, too—I don't want to become a burden to my kids. Consider this: The number of Americans aged 100 or older is projected to grow by more than 400 percent over the next three decades, with women making up an impressive 68 percent of that group.[25] When you think about how much money you'll need to secure your future, planning for a 100-year lifespan isn't just smart—it's imperative.

Know Your Vision

People create vision boards for their dream home, career, and even their ideal relationship. So why not do the same for your financial life? Reflecting on the work you did in chapter 4, let's explore your vision for your personal and professional futures. Maybe you dream of traveling more, starting a business, going back to school, gaining a credential to advance your career, giving back, making more money, or simply devoting more time to things that light you up. Perhaps your vision also includes something unexpected—a new hot tub or even a chance to raise chickens (who would have guessed this would become Ellen DeGeneres's post–talk show passion?).

What matters most is that you take the time to identify what's *truly* important to you and create action steps to help turn your vision into reality. As I set out to rebuild my life, there was so much uncertainty. Despite this, I had a clear vision of what I wanted for my future. And that vision became my guiding light—especially during those early dark days. I knew I wanted to turn my nightmare into something meaningful, something that could help other women understand the importance of financial independence and equip them with the resources to achieve it. I envisioned building a career around that mission—and eventually writing this book. However, back then I had never written anything beyond high school or college essays. I was all about math and science. English? Let's just say it wasn't exactly my forte—not by a longshot.

But I knew I had valuable experiences and advice to share, so I just started writing. I hired a copy editor who agreed to help me refine my raw skills, then I reached out to online platforms to see if they'd be interested in publishing my work. One day, after seeing Arianna Huffington speak on stage at a women's conference, I decided to take a bold step—I emailed her and asked if she'd consider letting me write for *The Huffington Post*.

Well, wouldn't you know it? She said *yes*!

Each piece I wrote helped me build confidence, and eventually I landed a gig as a paid monthly columnist for *Entrepreneur* magazine. Wait . . . what? That's right. Each small step led to another opportunity, reinforcing what I had begun to believe—I *was* a writer. That's how it works. Rome wasn't built in a day. But when you have a goal in mind, even the smallest baby steps can lead to big breakthroughs.

At the same time, I also pictured myself back in Texas, living in the Hill Country on a small ranch that would serve as our family hub—a place where my sons could always return and where we could create lifelong memories together. This was the dream Richard and I shared as young parents, and now I was determined to make it a reality on my own. It truly felt like nothing more than a pipe dream. But I cut a picture out from a magazine of a small house on a sprawling piece of land outside Fredericksburg, Texas, and pinned it to my vision board—a daily reminder of my wild, hairy aspiration.

Lastly, I set a concrete goal: to grow my wealth tenfold over the next eight years—from the moment my divorce was finalized until my 50th birthday. Today, I'm living proof of the incredible power of visualization. Because every single one of those visions became my reality.

Now, ask yourself: What do I want my life to look like in one year, five years, 10 years, and even 20? Dream big! Don't be afraid to set a few lofty goals. Because if you can dream it, you can achieve it! Next, make a list of three or four key aspects of that vision so you can start to identify the best ways to turn each of them into reality.

Think 45-20-35

Remember, there are *only* four ways to build wealth:

1. Invest the money you earn.
2. Invest in yourself (so you can earn more and ultimately save more).
3. Reinvest the money that is working for you.
4. Pay down debt—particularly the bad kind (high interest debt or the debt you used to purchase an underperforming or depreciating asset).

Since living beyond your means can sabotage your ability to do each, it's essential that you incorporate the 45-20-35 model into your new financial plan. Using the framework described in chapter 5, take a hard look at your current spending relative to your income and ask yourself:

* Am I currently **putting *less than* 45 percent** of my monthly inflows toward my unavoidables (e.g., housing, auto, utilities, insurance)?
    - If not, what changes do I need to make?
    - How can I potentially reduce my spending in one area to help pay for something else that is more of a priority?
* Am I consistently **investing *at least* 20 percent** of my monthly net income in my future?
    - If so, what am I currently doing with that money? Is it sitting in a bank account? Am I putting more toward my retirement savings? Am I paying down outstanding debt?
    - If not, what can I cut back on to start?
* What about the rest of my spending? Am I **spending *no more* than 35 percent** on everything else—groceries, gas, clothes, eating out with friends, manis, pedis, and even vet visits for pets?

- Am I relying on credit cards to cover a shortfall?
- Do I need to find ways to cut back to help fund more of my unavoidables? Or maybe make up for lost time by investing more than 20 percent in my future?
- Am I planning and saving for big-ticket items (e.g., a trip or a designer handbag) rather than paying for them all at once?

The 20 Percent

When it comes to your 20 percent, how it should be used is unique to you—it all depends on your current situation and goals. Having an emergency fund and paying off bad debt should be *everyone's* top two priorities, but knowing which one comes first can be tricky. On one hand, paying off debt might save you *a lot* of money in interest. On the other hand, not having a safety net for unexpected expenses could force you into more debt, potentially erasing any progress you've made.

My advice is this: If you're able to comfortably meet your minimum debt payments, your first priority should be to build an emergency fund that covers *at least* two months of expenses. Once that's done, begin to put more of your 20 percent toward paying off debt. And focus on the highest interest stuff first. Meanwhile, keep contributing—albeit a smaller amount—to your emergency fund until you have six months' worth of expenses. Once that's accomplished, your next priority, even over building your assets, should be eliminating all your bad debt. Why? Because the interest on that outstanding debt is likely higher than any future returns on those investments, especially if it's a credit card balance.

After you have a fully funded emergency fund and have eliminated all your bad debt, you can concentrate on other ways to increase your net worth, such as maximizing your retirement contributions, funding a brokerage account, saving to buy a rental property, or even investing in your personal development—like signing up for an online class, setting money aside to start a business, or hiring a life coach or job recruiter. The sky is the limit—the only caveat here is that whatever you put this money toward must work to build your long-term financial security.

The 35 Percent

Now let's dive deeper into your 35 percent. Remember, this is intended to be your empowerment money—it's the dollars you spend on food, clothing, or a few nights out with friends. And it fluctuates based on the decisions *you* make. This is the money you can take charge of and become more intentional with given your current priorities. Perhaps you need to increase your retirement savings beyond what you're doing from your 20 percent. Or maybe you've always wanted to cycle, so now you're saving to buy a bike. Both options might require you to say no to a few temptations and put those funds toward these new goals.

Warning: If you're currently spending more than 35 percent of your net income on these variable expenses, the reality is that you're likely relying on credit cards to fund any deficit. This can also happen if you are trying to save too much each month and consequently starving yourself of cash. And with the average card charging 24 percent interest in 2025, this will erode any return generated by your well-intended desire to save.

Typically, I operate under two spending approaches: First, there's my regular spending plan. Then, there's what I call "the financial cliff"—a backup plan where I know exactly which expenses I can immediately cut from my 35 percent if something unexpected comes up. That way, if an emergency arises, I can switch to this plan right away. This allows me to allocate part of my 35 percent to cover the surprise cost without impacting my ability to cover my unavoidables or continue to invest 20 percent in my future. The goal here is for you to live a life you can confidently afford—no matter what life throws your way.

Be Intentional with Your Assets

Every asset you own should serve a purpose. Your home, for example, puts a roof over your head, and your car helps you get from one place to another. Neither can do much of anything else until you sell them. Some investments are made only to generate income. Others (like retirement assets) are intended to grow exponentially until your golden years. Once you stop working, their purpose changes, shifting from an appreciating asset to an income source. The same goes for your saving account. The intent of that asset is to provide a safe place for your money so you can quickly access it when you're in a pinch.

The purpose of each asset should also determine how to invest those dollars and cents. Take, for example, a lump sum of cash you want to invest so it can help subsidize the money you'll have in retirement. Since your goal with it is long-term growth, you wouldn't want to put that money in a standard savings account, earning 0.8 percent interest— which also is far less than inflation. Unless, of course, you're my aunt, whom I absolutely adore. I recently learned that she's been doing just that for over 20 years. She has *always* struggled with her relationship with money. Her dominant money personalities are Penny Pincher and Avoider. In fact, even a subtle mention of the word *money* sends her into a panic. Her fear of losing money is so great that her emergency fund, the cash she's set aside to purchase a new car, and the money she's saved to supplement her teacher pension is all sitting in three different bank accounts, earning less than 1 percent a year. As it turns out, the only two investment vehicles she has ever used throughout her 77 years are savings accounts and CDs. And the opportunity cost of that decision is well into the millions.

Do you understand the current purpose of your assets and how each is currently working for you? Are you maximizing their earning power? Given your new goals, do you need to make any changes?

I am currently building a house. Two years ago, when I set this goal, I immediately turned to my balance sheet to figure out the best way to achieve it. Given my age, the current interest rate environment, and other goals I have for the next few years, I decided against taking on a large mortgage. Instead, I planned to use some of the money in my taxable investment accounts (i.e., nonretirement accounts) to help fund the construction—especially since I saw this as a good arbitrage opportunity. In my area, buyers are willing to pay a nice premium for a finished home rather than building one themselves. Although I had no plans to build and sell the house, I knew the value of my new home would be significantly higher than construction costs and what I paid for the lot, which would meaningfully increase my net worth. Plus, if I ever needed to access that money, I could sell the home and put the proceeds to work in a different way. This new house would provide a roof over my head, and it would be a good investment opportunity for me to capitalize on in the future.

At that time, however, those assets were invested with a growth objective in mind, aiming for substantial appreciation over the next 10 to 15 years. But now that my goal for some of those assets had changed, I needed to adjust how they were invested. As part of my planning, I allocated the funds needed for the project into a money market fund. And although this move would result in lower returns temporarily—until the house was complete—it gave me peace of mind knowing the money would be readily available when needed and not exposed to unnecessary risk.

So, as you work to build your plan, think about the purpose of each of your assets, including those you hope to own in the future. This can help you be more thoughtful around how best to use your assets to help accomplish your goals, which includes how those dollars need to be invested.

Establish Your Action Steps

Now let's pull everything together and map out your plan. To illustrate the best way to do this, allow me to introduce you to three women: Sue, a newly divorced woman who's rebuilding her life and rediscovering her independence; Elle, a young professional juggling her career aspirations and personal desires; and Kim, a married woman facing an unexpected crisis that's jeopardizing her family's financial security. I'll walk you through each woman's current financial reality, along with her goals, needs, and priorities. For each scenario, I'll break down the before and after and detail key steps in between that help get these three women on the right path. Although some assumptions may feel oversimplified, my goal is to highlight the financial impact of just a few changes. Along the way, I hope you'll have a few aha moments as you learn my methodology and realize just how much control you have over your money—and your future.

. . .

Meet Sue

Sue is a 51-year-old divorcée with two kids, John (18) and Jake (14). Sue lives in San Diego and is a nurse. While she loves her work, her other passion is yoga, and she's eager to start traveling to meet people and enjoy new experiences. The following is an overview of Sue's current financial situation, goals, and interests.

Sue's Snapshot

AGE 51, DIVORCED, TWO KIDS John (18), Jake (14)	**NET WORTH** $765,000
MONTHLY NET INCOME $7,417 Child support: $850 Spousal support: $1,800 Net salary: $4,767	**ASSETS** Cash: $25,000 Home: $800,000 Retirement: $150,000
GOALS Start a business, teach yoga	**DEBTS** Credit cards: $10,000 HELOC: $0 Mortgage: $200,000
PASSIONS Yoga, travel	**DESIRED RETIREMENT AGE** 70

Sue's Current Reality

Today, Sue's total monthly net income is just shy of $7,420. And while it looks to be diversified, the fact is 36 percent of it is dependent on her ex-husband. Given over half of custodial parents don't receive the full amount of what's owed to them each month,[26] replacing this income with another source to reduce her dependency on his ability to consistently pay her should be one of Sue's top priorities—because even if her ex-husband pays regularly, it won't last forever.

Although Sue has an impressive net worth of $765,000, nearly every single bit of it is illiquid. This means she essentially can't do anything with it without selling her home or liquidating some of her retirement accounts, which is a huge no-no, given the 10 percent early withdrawal penalty and tax Sue would face. The two combined could instantly turn that $150,000 account into just $80,000. Ouch! Speaking of her retirement savings, Sue recently learned after consulting with her benefits department that she isn't fully utilizing her annual 401(k) contribution limits, which is now $31,000 because she's over the age of 49.

Some good news: Sue has access to good debt—a $50,000 home equity line of credit (HELOC), which currently has a zero balance. Otherwise relying on her retirement accounts to fund an emergency might have been a necessity, especially since she currently doesn't have enough cash to cover six months' worth of living expenses, and she already has a significant amount of credit card debt. Another bright spot is that Sue doesn't plan to retire any time soon, so her money has almost 20 years to keep working for her.

Sue's Vision for the Future

Given Sue's love for yoga and need to prepare for the eventual loss of her child and spousal support income, she is eager to start teaching classes to supplement her earnings as a nurse. She's also looking for ways to meet new people and, frankly, a reason to get out of the house at night and on weekends.

With her youngest son, Jake, graduating from high school in less than four years, Sue knows an empty nest is right around the corner. Consequently, she's already begun looking for a travel group to join and making a list of the countries she wants to visit. Sue pictures herself running her own yoga studio, where she can train other teachers and build a vibrant yoga community. She's always wanted to start her own business but never thought she'd have the opportunity.

Sue's 45-20-35 Model

A Framework for Sue's Total Monthly Expenses

Adjusted Net Monthly Income of $6,375
Current Child and Spousal Support Plus Current Net Salary
Minus Additional 401(k) Contributions

No more than 45% *Unavoidable Expenses*	At least 20% *Non-Negotiable Expenses*		No more than 35% *Empowerment Money*	
$2,869	**$1,275**		**$2,231**	
	Cash savings	$375	Travel fund	$300
	Investment fund	$600		
	Teacher training	$300		

Sue's Action Steps

Given her current financial reality, vision for her future, and the 45-20-35 framework, Sue's immediate action steps include the following:

1. **Maximize her retirement savings.** She plans to immediately increase her monthly 401(k) contributions by $1,500 and consistently save until she retires. Although this will reduce her paycheck by $1,042 (the difference from $1,500 is due to the tax benefit), leaving her with $3,725. She believes the sacrifice is worthwhile; the additional monthly contribution could add nearly $800,000 to her wealth over the next two decades.

2. **Pay down bad debt.** She plans to take $10,000 from her savings account and immediately pay off her credit cards, leaving her with $15,000 remaining in that account.

3. **Establish an emergency fund.** Sue knows that while she doesn't need to use it now, her HELOC is available to supplement

her savings, effectively creating a $65,000 emergency fund. This gives her peace of mind, knowing she has enough to cover 12 months of expenses in case of an unexpected crisis.

4. **Reduce monthly expenses.** With her net income reduced, Sue needs to find ways to cut her monthly overhead. One option, depending on the current interest rates, is to refinance her $200,000 mortgage. This could significantly lower her monthly payment, especially since her current payments are based on her original $425,000 loan. Doing so might help her reach the 45 percent target for her unavoidables. It would free up some of her 35 percent empowerment money, which she's frequently had to use to fund her monthly deficit. This would allow her to use some of those funds to build a travel fund for future adventures.

5. **Diversify into more liquid investments.** Sue plans to allocate $600 each month from her 20 percent into an investment account, targeting a 7 percent return. Additionally, she will save another $375 a month to grow her savings account. She hopes both will help her begin to feel more secure about starting her business.

6. **Invest in her future.** Lastly, Sue plans to invest the balance of her 20 percent in herself. Her goal: get certified to teach yoga, which will help her land a side gig and earn extra money.

Sue's Results

As a result of these six simple steps, within one year Sue:

* Has no credit card debt
* Has a plan to cover any emergency expenses with nearly $20,000 in savings and access to an additional $50,000 if needed
* Saved $3,600 in a travel fund and is heading to Costa Rica with a group of friends

* Invested an additional $18,000 in her retirement account

* Is building her liquid assets and diversifying, with nearly $7,500 now in a brokerage account

* Completed her yoga training certification and is now teaching classes three nights a week

* Is focused on increasing her income today to ensure she's well prepared when her support payments end

* Feels much more empowered by her financial situation and confident in her decisions moving forward

Here is where it gets *really* interesting: In 20 years those same six steps—nothing more, nothing less—could increase her net worth by about 314 percent! And this doesn't even include any money Sue might generate from owning her yoga studio.

Sue's Results

BEFORE		AFTER	
CURRENT NET WORTH		**PROJECTED NET WORTH AT 70**	
Cash *(less credit card debt)*	$15,000	Cash	$100,000
Retirement accounts	$150,000	Investment accounts	$228,000
Equity in home	$600,000	Retirement accounts	$1,790,000
TOTAL: $765,000		Equity in home	$1,052,000
		TOTAL: $3,170,000*	

An increase of 314%

---

* Estimated inflation-adjusted annual growth: 3 percent real estate, 5 percent investment, 7 percent retirement. Note: Calculations do not reflect transaction costs or taxes.

How is this growth possible? It all goes back to opportunity cost and compounding. By making intentional choices with her money and maximizing its earning power and liquidity, Sue has built a nice nest egg for retirement. When Sue decides to stop working and begins relying on her wealth to fund her lifestyle—particularly if she chooses to sell her house, rent a home, and reinvest the equity into another asset—she'll be able to afford her desired lifestyle.

A good rule of thumb is that for every $40,000 worth of annual expenses, you'll need $1,000,000 of investable assets. This is called the 4 percent rule: a tool used to determine how much you can comfortably take from your investable assets each year to fund your retirement. By pulling out only 4 percent of your portfolio's value annually and allowing the rest of your investments to grow, you can budget a safe withdrawal indefinitely. This is especially important in your 50s and 60s, since you may need your savings to last another 30 to 40 years. As you continue to age, preserving the principal balance of your investments becomes less critical because your risk of running out of money decreases.

Using the 4 percent rule, if we assume Sues uses the full $3.17 million to fund her retirement, she can comfortably withdraw up to $126,000 a year. All of this goes to show that Sue will be in a much better spot at 70 because she took these six steps instead of doing nothing.

I understand that the 4 percent rule might seem overwhelming, but keep in mind that your financial needs typically decrease as you age. Over time, you'll likely spend less each month. While healthcare costs may rise, you're also less likely to be accumulating possessions or supporting family members in the same way you may have when you were younger. Consider the house you're living in right now—downsizing or even renting in retirement could allow you to tap your home's equity as another source of funds. Beyond that, most retirees have multiple sources of income to help cover their monthly expenses, including Social

Security, pensions, and rental income. With proper planning, funding your golden years can be more manageable than it might seem today.

• • •

Meet Elle

Elle is a 29-year-old single woman who lives in Chicago. Elle is an art director at a marketing agency who is viewed by all as a rising star. Her passions are art and long-distance running. She ran track in college and misses the competition, so now she has started training for triathlons. The following is an overview of Elle's current financial situation, goals, and interests.

Elle's Snapshot

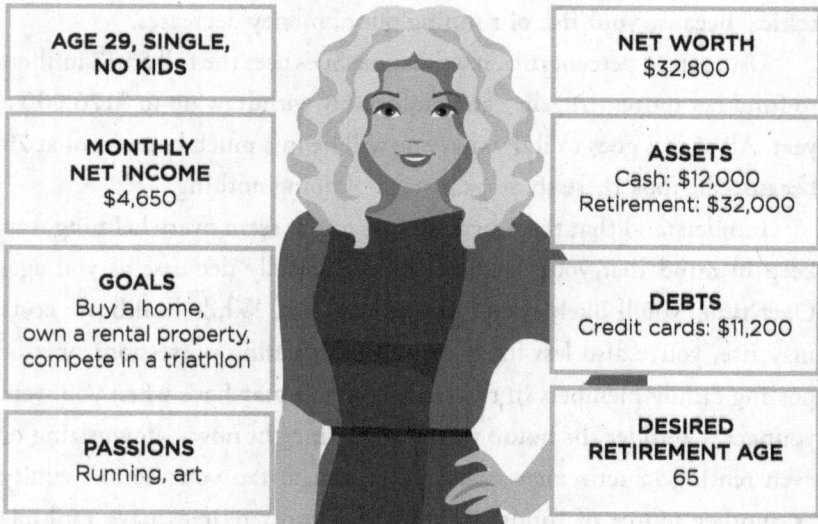

AGE 29, SINGLE, NO KIDS

NET WORTH
$32,800

MONTHLY NET INCOME
$4,650

ASSETS
Cash: $12,000
Retirement: $32,000

GOALS
Buy a home,
own a rental property,
compete in a triathlon

DEBTS
Credit cards: $11,200

PASSIONS
Running, art

DESIRED RETIREMENT AGE
65

Elle's Current Reality

Elle earns $75,000 a year, which translates to an after-tax income of $4,650 per month. This is her only source of income. While many of her friends have turned to side gigs to keep up with the rising cost of living, Elle had never considered it—until now. She is struggling to stretch her dollars to cover her monthly expenses, and she's beginning to explore her options.

Her net worth is just over $32,000, which takes into consideration her hefty credit card debt. Unfortunately, that balance keeps climbing. Elle tends to rely on her cards when she's short on cash each month. She needs a plan to get those paid off and build an appropriate emergency fund—especially since her only other asset outside of her savings account is her 401(k).

Elle has been contributing roughly $3,000 annually to her retirement plan. At this level she is not taking full advantage of her employer contribution benefits. Fortunately, she can still make up for lost time because she has 36 years until retirement if she retires at 65.

Elle's Vision for the Future

Elle understands that, given her age and current circumstance, a lot could change in the next few years. With that in mind, she has just three primary goals. First, Elle is eager to start competing in triathlons and dreams of buying a purpose-built triathlon bike, which could cost up to $10,000. Due to her current financial situation, this feels like a pipe dream. Next, given her love of art, Elle hopes to return to knife painting in her spare time and explore other mediums, such as sculpture and mixed media. Last, Elle aspires to purchase a condo in the West Loop, where the price for a one-bedroom currently ranges from $400,00 to $500,000. She sees this as a potential investment opportunity, with the option to rent it out in the future.

Elle's 45-20-35

A Framework for Elle's Total Monthly Expenses

Adjusted Net Monthly Income of $4,550

Current Net Salary Minus Additional 401(k) Contributions

No more than 45% *Unavoidable Expenses*	At least 20% *Non-Negotiable Expenses*	No more than 35% *Empowerment Money*
$2,048	$910	$1,592
	Year 1: Emergency fund $410 Debt reduction $500	
	Year 2: Emergency fund $910	
	Year 3 & Beyond: Investment account $910	

Elle's Action Steps

Given her current financial reality, vision for her future, and the 45-20-35 framework, Elle's immediate action steps include the following:

1. **Increase her retirement savings.** Elle plans to increase her annual 401(k) contribution by $1,500 to $4,500. By saving an extra $125 a month, Elle will ensure she receives the full 6 percent employer matching contribution.* While this adjustment will reduce her monthly net income by around $100 to $4,550 (the difference from $125 is due to the tax benefit), with over three decades for her investments to grow, it could potentially add nearly $490,000 to her retirement savings. How? Her company matches the additional $125 monthly contribution,

---

* A common 401(k) employer matching program is a 1:1 match up to 6 percent of your gross income. Since Elle's total annual contribution is exactly 6 percent, her company is matching 100 percent of her $4,500 annual contribution.

so effectively, she's investing a total of $250 per month. When compounded at a 7 percent annual return over 36 years, this can generate some serious results.

2. **Pay down bad debt.** Elle plans to use $5,000 from her savings and pay down part of her credit card balance. Additionally, she'll put $500 per month toward paying off the remaining debt, which should take about a year.

3. **Build an emergency fund.** She will allocate the remaining $7,000 of her savings to an emergency fund and contribute the balance of her 20 percent ($410 a month) to it while she's working to pay off her credit card debt. Once that debt is gone, she will put the full $910 each month toward her emergency fund for an additional 12 months. This approach will help her build up nearly $23,000 by the end of the second year of the plan to cover her expenses in case the unexpected happens.

4. **Diversify her assets.** Once Elle is debt-free and has a well-funded emergency fund, she plans to invest her entire 20 percent ($910 per month) into a brokerage account. This will help her build wealth beyond her retirement assets and save for a future down payment on a house.

5. **Diversify her income.** Lastly, she's exploring a side hustle to both supplement and diversify her income. A local gallery is interested in representing her art, and Elle is also interviewing at a local junior college for a part-time graphic design teaching position.

Elle's Results

As a result of these five simple steps, within one year Elle:

* Is debt-free
* Has $12,000 to cover an unexpected event and is on track to have $23,000 in her emergency fund by the end of the following year

* Has a plan to invest $11,000 per year in non-retirement assets
* Has a new goal of buying a home by the time she is 35
* Is focused on increasing her income so she can start saving for a new bike and boost her retirement savings by opening a Roth IRA
* Feels much more empowered by her financial situation and confident in her decisions

But check this out: In 36 years those same five steps—nothing more, nothing less—could increase her net worth by almost 8,600 percent! And this assumes Elle never makes more than $75,000 per year.

Elle's Results

BEFORE		AFTER	
CURRENT NET WORTH		PROJECTED NET WORTH AT 65	
Cash (less credit card debt)	$800	Cash	$23,000
Retirement accounts	$32,000	Investment accounts	$973,000
TOTAL: $32,800		Retirement accounts	$1,853,000
		Future equity in home	TBD
		Future Roth IRA	TBD
		TOTAL: $2,849,000*	

An increase of 8,586%

Again, it's all thanks to the power of opportunity cost and compounding! Using the 4 percent rule, if we assume Elle uses the full $2.85 million to fund her retirement, she can comfortably withdraw up to

---

* Estimated inflation-adjusted annual growth: 3 percent real estate, 5 percent investment, 7 percent retirement. Note: Calculations do not reflect transaction costs or taxes.

$114,000 a year without the risk of outliving her money. That's nearly $40,000 more than she made working. It's a great example of how money can have more earning power than us when we put enough of it to work!

. . .

Meet Kim

Kim is a married 59-year-old with two kids, Grace (31) and Kate (25). Kim and her husband, John, live in a suburb of Dallas. Recently John was severely injured in a car accident and is on disability. Kim was an immigration attorney but left the workforce almost 25 years ago when her daughter, Kate, was a year old. Given John's accident, Kim knows she needs to go back to work. The following is an overview of Kim's current financial situation, goals, and interests.

Kim's Snapshot

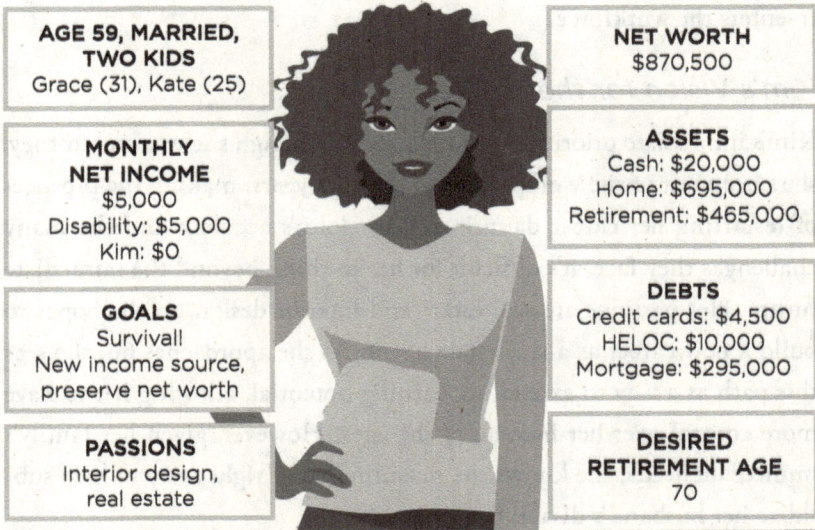

AGE 59, MARRIED, TWO KIDS Grace (31), Kate (25)	**NET WORTH** $870,500
MONTHLY NET INCOME $5,000 Disability: $5,000 Kim: $0	**ASSETS** Cash: $20,000 Home: $695,000 Retirement: $465,000
GOALS Survival! New income source, preserve net worth	**DEBTS** Credit cards: $4,500 HELOC: $10,000 Mortgage: $295,000
PASSIONS Interior design, real estate	**DESIRED RETIREMENT AGE** 70

Kim's Current Reality

Kim and her husband are facing financial challenges due to his long-term disability, which currently provides a net income of $5,000 per month. Since he may be able to work in some capacity in the future, he does not qualify for Social Security disability benefits. Unfortunately, their emergency fund is likely not sufficient to cover their immediate financial needs. However, they do have access to an additional $40,000 through their home equity line of credit (HELOC), which could serve as a temporary financial cushion until Kim is able to find a job.

One of the biggest concerns is that John's disability income is not enough to cover their monthly expenses. Adding to the issue, nearly all their assets are illiquid, meaning they cannot easily access cash without either selling their home or tapping into their retirement accounts—and the latter should be avoided at all costs. Given these constraints, preserving their assets must be a top priority. With at least 11 years before reaching retirement age, Kim and John have a critical window to grow their assets and improve their financial situation. This timeline could extend even further, depending on Kim's earning potential when she re-enters the workforce.

Kim's Vision for the Future

Kim's immediate priority is finding a job. Although she was an attorney, she's been out of the workplace for nearly 25 years, making the prospect of restarting her career daunting. With John's accident and the many challenges they face, it's difficult for her to think beyond the immediate future. Her passions are real estate and interior design, so she hopes to build a new career as a real estate agent. As she approaches 60, she sees this path as a way to extend her earning potential, allowing her to have more control over her income as she ages. However, given her family's immediate needs, she knows she must find work right away to help subsidize her husband's disability income.

Kim's 45-20-35

A Framework for Kim's Total Monthly Expenses

Current Net Monthly Income of $5,000

No more than 45% *Unavoidable Expenses*	At least 20% *Non-Negotiable Expenses*	No more than 35% *Empowerment Money*
$2,250	**$1,000**	**$1,750**
	Put toward UNAVOIDABLES $625	All spending must focus
	Future career fund $375	on UNAVOIDABLES and additional NEEDS

Future Net Monthly Income of $10,533
John's Disability Payment Plus Kim's New Net Salary

No more than 45% *Unavoidable Expenses*	At least 20% *Non-Negotiable Expenses*	No more than 35% *Empowerment Money*
$4,740	**$2,106**	**$3,687**
	Emergency fund $606	
	New retirement savings $1,000	
	Future career fund $500	

Kim's Plan

Given Kim and John's current financial reality, vision for the future, and the 45-20-35 framework, Kim's immediate action steps include:

1. **Secure stable employment.** Kim is hopeful she'll secure a job as an attorney advisor for US Citizenship and Immigration Services. This role would provide excellent medical and retirement benefits while adding $5,533 to their monthly net income.

2. **Sell their home.** Although it's an incredibly emotional and difficult decision given how attached Kim, John, and their daughters are to their home, they plan to sell it and move into a rental. While finding a place that will accommodate John's condition might be challenging and slightly more expensive than expected, renting will still be more cost effective than retrofitting their current house. Additionally, they need access to cash just in case John's condition deteriorates and his needs change.

3. **Pay off bad debt and build an emergency fund.** Kim and John will use $4,500 from savings to pay off their credit card debt and set aside the remaining $15,500 as an emergency fund. After their home sells, they'll allocate an additional $20,000 from the proceeds—bringing their total emergency fund savings to $35,500. Once Kim secures employment, they plan to contribute $606 per month until their emergency fund reaches $70,000—enough to cover eight months of their living expenses.

4. **Lower monthly expenses.** They intend to sell their luxury sedan and use a small portion of the proceeds from the home sale to buy a used car that better accommodates John's needs. Eliminating a car payment will save them over $650 a month while also lowering their auto insurance premium.

5. **Increase liquidity.** They plan to invest $339,000 of the home sale proceeds to maximize their assets' earning power while maintaining financial flexibility.

6. **Invest in her future.** Kim will allocate $375 per month toward her future real estate career, initially covering the cost of earning her real estate license. Additionally, she'll start connecting with brokers to identify the best fit for her long-term career goals. Once employed, Kim plans to continue to build this savings account and use it to invest in her future real estate business. These funds will help offset income loss when she

transitions from a W2 salary to a commission-based career. It will also cover start-up costs such as website, advertising, and marketing expenses.

7. **Grow their retirement savings.** Since John can no longer contribute to a 401(k) and Kim will eventually be self-employed, they each plan to contribute $500 per month to a Roth IRA account. This will allow them to continue growing their retirement savings and maintain long-term financial security.

Kim's Results

As a result of just these seven steps, within one year Kim and John:

* Increased their monthly net income by $5,533, thanks to Kim's new job. However, to make ends meet during the first six months after John's accident and before Kim was employed, they had to borrow an additional $16,000 from their HELOC. This debt was paid off immediately after selling their home.

* Have nearly $40,000 in their emergency fund and nearly $4,000 in a designated account for Kim's future business.

* Have over $350,000 in an investment account, which is now positioned to grow while also serving as a secondary safety net to supplement their emergency fund if John experiences a major setback requiring additional medical support.

* Avoided tapping into their retirement savings during their crisis and are now consistently contributing an extra $1,000 per month toward their future.

Now, take a look at this! In just 11 years, those same seven steps—once again, nothing more, nothing less—could increase their net worth by over 110 percent! And that's without factoring in any additional savings or investments once Kim transitions to her new career. Now imagine if they kept the status quo, sold the house, and used the proceeds to help cover their monthly living expenses. They'd likely be left relying solely on retirement assets when they reached 70, which could end up being half of what they could have built by following their seven-step plan.

Kim's Results

BEFORE		AFTER	
CURRENT NET WORTH		**PROJECTED NET WORTH AT 70**	
Cash *(less credit card debt)*	$15,500	Cash	$70,000
Retirement accounts	$465,000	Investment accounts	$580,000
Equity in home	$390,000	Retirement accounts	$1,200,000
TOTAL: $870,500		**TOTAL: $1,850,000***	

An increase of 113%

• • •

Reflecting on these three different scenarios, what are your takeaways? What surprised you the most? More importantly, are you ready to take action? I hope that you're starting to see that time is money—and you simply can't afford to do nothing.

Now it's your turn! Let's create a clear picture of the key steps you should take to build the life you envision. To better understand your current financial situation and start planning for your future, reflect

---

* Estimated inflation-adjusted annual growth: 3 percent real estate, 5 percent investment, 7 percent retirement. Note: Calculations do not reflect transaction costs or taxes.

on the questions provided throughout this chapter. Your answers will help you identify what actions are needed to turn your vision into reality. The framework below will guide you in creating your personal financial road map.

And once you have a plan, it's time to execute, execute, execute!

Your Financial Road Map

TARGET MONTHLY EXPENSES ON $_____ NET MONTHLY INCOME

<45% PER MONTH IN UNAVOIDABLE EXPENSES

$_____

Housing (30%) $_____

Transportation (5%) $_____

Utilities (5%) $_____

Insurance (5%) $_____

>20% PER MONTH IN NON-NEGOTIABLE EXPENSES

$_____

Emergency fund savings $_____

Debt reduction $_____

Retirement contribution $_____

Investment savings $_____

Other:_____ $_____

Other:_____ $_____

*Note: Please complete the above section based on
your needs and goals for the future.*

<35% PER MONTH IN EMPOWERMENT MONEY

$_____

Consists of needs and wants (groceries, clothing, eating out, etc.)
Your spending fluctuates based on the decisions YOU make every day.

Your Financial Road Map

(CONTINUED)

YOUR INITIAL ACTION PLAN

1. _____
   _____
   _____

2. _____
   _____
   _____

3. _____
   _____
   _____
   _____

4. _____
   _____
   _____

5. _____
   _____
   _____

6. _____
   _____
   _____

Chapter Eight
Step Five—Stay the Course

> *Your daily actions determine your*
> *future. Make each one count.*
> —Unknown

We've all experienced it: the rush of excitement that comes with setting a new goal. But then reality sets in, and we quickly lose our mojo. This is the "knowing but not doing" phenomenon—the disconnect between what we know we need to do and actually doing it, like knowing you should eat healthy but still indulging in a pint of ice cream, or knowing you should save money but still splurging on that new dress. This predicament isn't just about personal weakness or lack of willpower. The truth is that for most of us, the gap between knowledge and action is deeply rooted in our mindset. In other words, the secret to success lies within the six inches between our ears.

Pushing yourself beyond your self-defined limitations—such as fear of failure, struggles with self-doubt, and dread of judgment—can be downright scary and incredibly uncomfortable. But trust me when I say that icky sensation is actually a good sign: Discomfort means you're growing. So, if you are ready to make real changes—financially and emotionally—in your life and stay the course, you need to lean in and get comfortable with the uncomfortable.

Here are a few key ways to help you do this. First, put your new intentions out into the world! Whether you're aiming to be debt-free, land a new job, or simply have a better handle on what you spent last month, share your goals with a friend, mentor, or family member who can help hold you accountable. Voicing your aspirations can transform your vision into tangible commitments. And if you find someone on a similar journey, that's even better! You can support each other, tackle challenges together, and celebrate one another's wins.

Next, try creating visual reminders of what you want to accomplish using images or words that inspire or encourage you. My bathroom mirror, for example, is filled with bold colored sticky notes that say "Think big," "If you can dream it, you can achieve it," "Be calm, be strong, be grateful," and my personal favorite, "Those voices inside your head are lying." Additionally, remember to start small with your actions. When it comes to how you manage your money daily, focus on the practical steps you can take to:

* Stay connected to your money and your goals
* Create a smart approach to daily financial decisions
* Spot blind spots and avoid money traps

Throughout this chapter, I will share ideas and best practices to help you achieve all three. Doing so will build momentum and confidence, allowing you to be more strategic with your wealth and turn the vision you have for your future into reality. And as you incorporate these new actions into your daily routine, remember that it takes about 21 days for something to become a habit. So, commit to them, practice consistently, and repeat, repeat, repeat. And finally, be gentle with yourself. We're all perfectly imperfect. You'll encounter setbacks, but each one is a learning opportunity and a vital part of your success—so stay the course!

Stay Connected to Your Money and Your Goals

Despite our best efforts and carefully crafted plans, a staggering 84 percent of us still end up overspending each month.[27] One major reason? We lose touch with our daily money habits. The best way to tackle this is to schedule a weekly money date. Of course, when I suggest to women that they make a date with their money, I often get a few raised eyebrows. But just as you set aside time for date night with your partner to focus on each other, you need to regularly focus on your money—both as an individual and as a couple, if you're partnered. It's about making your financial health a priority, not an afterthought.

You might be thinking, *I got this; I'm good to go! I already use a budgeting app to track my finances regularly.* But here's the thing: relying solely on an app can create a false sense of control—and cause you to overlook other financial saboteurs, like fraud or identity theft. In fact, sticking to old-school methods and physically engaging with your money is often more effective than depending entirely on technology. Spending just 15 to 30 minutes each week connecting with your money will help you:

* Build self-awareness and accountability around all your money habits—the good, the bad, and the ugly.
* Quickly identify wasteful spending so you can proactively change course. Most people who track their spending typically do so at the end of the month, only to discover they've completely blown their budget, leaving them feeling utterly defeated.

* Be mindful of your daily, weekly, and monthly goals and track your progress.
* Identify inaccurate credit card charges—you can't believe how common this is.
* Minimize damage caused by unwelcome surprises, including, but not limited to, fraud and identity theft (I speak from personal experience here).

Your Money Date

THE PROCESS

1. Set aside 15 to 30 minutes of uninterrupted time each week for your money date. (For me, it's Saturday morning, lounging in bed with a cup of coffee.)

2. Equip yourself with a computer, paper, pen, and calculator.

3. Log in to your bank and credit card accounts and make note of current balances. Look for any low balances and make appropriate transfers, as needed.

4. Take a hard look at all transactions.

5. Double-check all debit card transactions. Make sure there are no surprises!

6. Identify any online payments and/or checks that have cleared—yes, some of us still pay for things the old-fashioned way.

7. Make note of all online payments and/or checks that have not cleared. Be sure to deduct those amounts from the current balance you documented when you first logged in. This is called your adjusted balance.

Your Money Date

8. If your adjusted balance is too low—or even negative—make appropriate transfers to avoid overdraft fees.

9. Examine all credit card transactions and add up all purchases you made that week. Confirm that all transactions were actually yours!

10. Review all your accounts—including subscription services and medical bills—to ensure there are no errors. These mistakes are more common than you might think—for example, a shocking 80 percent of medical bills in the United States contain inaccuracies.[28]

11. If you're not using a credit monitoring service like Experian, LifeLock, or Credit Karma, now's a good time to start. These tools can help catch identity theft early— before serious damage occurs. In 2021, one in 20 Americans was affected, with losses averaging $1,500.[29] Yet 60 percent didn't discover the fraud until three months or more had passed.[30]

CREDIT SCORE **710**

12. Now, take a moment to reflect and write down your observations.

✔ Did you see any unhealthy habits or patterns in your spending?

✔ Did you fall into any money traps—those unexpected situations or habits that can lead to financial loss? (I'll go into more detail on this later in the chapter.)

✔ What surprised you the most?

✔ Celebrate your highs and acknowledge your lows. And don't beat yourself up—all of this takes practice.

✔ What adjustments can you make to improve things before your next money date?

In March 2020, as if the onset of the pandemic wasn't enough, I was hit with a major surprise—and not the good kind: a blemished credit rating. There is little that will create more anxiety for a finance guru than this. During one of my weekly money check-ins, I logged into my Experian account and discovered a massive (and I mean *massive*!) drop in my credit score. I grabbed the phone and began dialing for answers.

Had my fear of falling victim to identity theft suddenly become a reality? Not exactly. It turns out that the man who once was my everything stopped making payments—not just for one month, but for three—on a student loan debt for one of our sons, and he neglected to let me know. This was a loan I had cosigned years earlier. (Why did I cosign a loan with my ex? It's a long story, not a wise decision on my part, and one I hope no one repeats.) As a result, I was now the proud owner of an additional $60,000 debt and a credit score that was nearly 200 points lower than it was just one month before. After I screamed out every four-letter word, I took action. Although damaging, the situation would have been far worse without my money date.

And your investment accounts? They call for a different approach—one that takes a longer-term perspective. It's easy to get caught up in the daily ups and downs of the market, especially with all the noise from the news and social media, but trust me: panic selling and FOMO (fear of missing out) buying based on any short-term movements are never a good idea. The market can be volatile, but history has shown that the long-term trend remains upward, despite even sharp declines. The key is to stay focused and avoid making decisions driven by emotions. Therefore, checking in on your investment accounts once a month is more than enough. Then, sit back, relax, and let them do their thing!

Create a Smart Approach
to Daily Financial Decisions

After all these years, I *still* get anxious about spending money on "just for fun" purchases. In fact, as I wrote this, I was freaking out about the $2,200 I had just put on my credit card for a flight to England to vacation with a new friend. I'd always dreamed of visiting London, especially Buckingham Palace, the British Museum, and, of course, Harrods.

The truth is, as a single mom of three boys, I hadn't taken a vacation on my own in nearly 13 years. Raising them after my divorce was hard enough, but doing it every day, 365 days a year, with all my energy focused on their emotional, physical, and financial needs, was beyond exhausting. I had already put two kids through college, and Drew was about to start his sophomore year. And while I still faced three more years of that financial obligation, the idea of stepping away for a little while—to explore and see the world through a new lens—felt like a long-awaited reprieve. A trip to London seemed like the start of an entirely new chapter, one where I could begin to prioritize me for the first time in over a decade.

Yet, I kept waking up in a panic, thinking of 101 reasons why I should cancel: Drew's college tuition was due, I needed new tires for my car, I had just spent a fortune at the vet—the list went on and on. But if I canceled, I'd miss out on a fabulous experience and priceless memories—plus my new friend might never speak to me again. Each of these things meant more to me than saving that $2,200. Sometimes the intrinsic value of one thing is worth more than the monetary value of another.

So, guess what? I went!

It all comes down to opportunity cost—the idea that saying yes to one thing means saying no to another. It's about weighing both the quantitative and qualitative value of each option in your financial decision-making. Over the next three months, before you buy something, ask yourself:

* Will the good, service, or experience fundamentally make my life better?
* Is there a more cost-effective alternative that could provide the same benefit?

Then, mentally calculate what that money could do for your net worth if you simply said no to the nonessential and invested it instead. And to do this, I suggest you use the Rule of 72.

Also, be mindful of *how* you spend. Personally, I recommend using cash—especially when you're building new money habits into your daily routine. And finally, shift your mindset: Turn saving into a game. You might be surprised at how fun it feels to win.

The Rule of 72

The Rule of 72 is a quick and easy formula to help estimate investment results by understanding how long it will take for your money to double at certain rates of return.

$$\textit{The Rule of 72} \quad \frac{72}{\text{Rate of Return}} = \frac{\text{Time for}}{\text{Investments}} \text{ to Double}$$

For instance, if you expect a 7 percent return, it will take about 10 years for your investment to double; at 5 percent, about 15 years, and so on. When you begin to do this for two, 10, or even 20 nonessentials, the impact of the Rule of 72 on each can really add up! This isn't about self-deprivation. It's about being more intentional with your spending so can feel confident about the decisions you make. And the way you make those purchases is just as important as the dollars you spend.

Cash Is Queen

We are a nation of overconsumers. We want what we want, and we want it now. And the convenience of using digital payments over cash makes it easier for us to get it. Think about it: What's less painful—sputting down a credit card or handing over a $100 bill? In fact, the average person is twice as likely to say yes to an impulse purchase when using a card over cash.[31]

Take a trip to HomeGoods. The check-out line is packed with gadgets—everything from body scrubs and nail care kits to silicone baking mats and reusable straws. You can even grab a pasta kit for dinner on your way to the register. And all of this is strategically placed to tempt you to spend more. When your default method of payment is plastic, it's a lot easier to fall into this trap. Yet using cash to defend yourself from such tactics is becoming harder and harder to do. How many times have you walked into a fast-food restaurant or approached the self-checkout at the grocery store only to see a sign that says "Card Only"? Add Amazon, Apple Pay, and Venmo to the mix, and it's no wonder the average credit card debt per person in 2024 was at an all-time high.[32]

The system sets us up to fail. And with the rise of digital money, this problem will only worsen. My advice: Ditch your credit cards, keep your phone in your pocket, and go back to the basics. Make cash queen. Cash is tangible. It's harder to part with dollar bills than with phantom money. And if you're like me, you'll focus much more on the cost of something when you use it.

So, here's my suggestion: For the next 30 days, withdraw enough cash to cover your 35 percent and commit to making it last as long as possible—because once it's gone, it's gone. Be mindful about when you make withdrawals. I found that Mondays were better than Fridays, as the risk of spending it all by Sunday night was just too great. I also used an envelope system, dividing the lump sum of cash into smaller categories: one for groceries, one for dining out, one for gasoline, one for entertainment, and so on. I managed those envelopes accordingly, rationing where needed based on priorities and goals.

I even created a special envelope for Chick-fil-A, given my youngest son's chicken nugget addiction. I kept it in the glove compartment of my car. Whenever he asked for an eight-pack, fries, and a vanilla shake, I handed him the envelope and asked, "Do you have enough? Because once it's gone, there won't be any nuggets for the rest of the week." This approach got him invested in the system, helping him see the actual dollars disappearing just as much as I did.

I'm not suggesting you adopt an all-cash policy forever—let's be real, our ever-growing cashless society would make that virtually impossible to do. Plus, all those rewards points can really stack up. When you do start using plastic again, try sticking to just one credit card and pay it off at the end of each day. While it may not be the same as using cash, it will still help you keep a close eye on the impact of your money habits.

Make It a Game

Beyond adopting an all-cash policy for a while, try taking on a few money challenges to help you pause before you spend. Think of it as a game—a fun way to become more mindful and intentional with your money on a daily basis.

Challenge 1: The 7-Day Rule

Sure, that owl-shaped lamp is adorable, but how badly do you really want (or need) it? Try waiting a week before you buy. If you still can't stop thinking about it, it might be worth the splurge. But most of those fleeting desires? It's amazing how often they simply fade away.

For the next three months, pledge to wait seven days before making an impulse purchase, and you'll start to see the distinction between your wants and your needs. To help me do this, I keep a note on my phone with a section for my wants and a section for my needs. When something catches my eye that I am tempted to buy, I jot it down and revisit it one week later. More times than I can count, I've looked at my list and thought, *What was I ever thinking?*

In fact, very few items ever make it to my needs list, and even then, after a week of reflection, I often realize I can make do with what I already have. It's eye-opening to see how little we actually need when we step back and give ourselves some time. This technique has helped me cut down on unnecessary spending and prioritize the things that mean the most to me. Like my floating glass desk—which is where I sat day after day to write this book, over a decade after I bought it. I vividly remember eyeing this treasure during one of my web-surfing sessions about a year after my divorce. Not only was it a super cool design, but I also had the perfect spot for it in my bedroom. It would be an awesome place to sit and write. But with a price tag of several hundred dollars and a backlog of bills still to tackle, I knew I really couldn't afford it. So I resisted. Yet I found myself thinking about that damn desk not just after seven days but even after seven months. This made me realize it was likely something worth saving for. So, I set aside a small portion of my 35 percent empowerment money until I had enough to buy it. And today, that desk means more to me than just a piece of furniture—it reminds me of what it took to earn it.

Challenge 2: Try a Spend-Free Weekend

From sundown on Friday night to sunup the following Monday, resist all temptations to spend. See what you can do during that time that *doesn't* cost money. Go for a nature walk or hike, jump on a bike, check out a free museum, volunteer your time to help a cause or friend, read a book, paint a picture, have a picnic. Get creative because there are many more free options than you think. Encourage your entire family to join in—even unplugging from their devices. What you'll gain from playing cards, having a Monopoly marathon, cooking, or watching a movie together might be worth far more than anything money can buy.

Challenge 3: Cut the Waste

A friend's 21-year-old son does this as a side hustle: He tells friends to give him all their monthly bills—cable, internet, cell phone—and haggles down all the prices or cuts out unused services altogether. It's a game for him.

And it could be a useful game for you, too.

Here is how to play: Go straight to your 45 percent unavoidables and start dialing your service providers for things like your cell phone, internet, television, home security, pest control, and lawn care. Then, start negotiating! But don't stop there—getting strategic with your insurance can lead to significant savings, especially in today's environment. With soaring premiums driven by a dramatic increase in claims over the last year, many experts advise resisting the urge to file claims to help ensure your policies will continue to be renewed.

I live in Texas, for example, which is one of the top five states with the highest premiums and among the top three for nonrenewal rates. It would take one heck of a disaster for me to even consider filing a claim. As a result, I've strategically raised my deductible to lower my monthly payment. Afterall, given the likelihood that I can't use my insurance for a hailstorm or if a tree crashes into my roof, I might as well pay as little as possible for coverage.

Bottom line: Invest the time to dig into the details, ask questions, and look for ways to get the services you need, but for as little out of pocket as possible. Your monthly savings might just leave you surprised.

Spot Blind Spots and Avoid Money Traps

When I was still living in California, before moving to Texas, the last thing I expected as I drove up the freeway from San Diego to Los Angeles was to fall into a money trap. Traffic? Yes. Frustration and delays? Naturally. But a money trap—those sneaky situations that unexpectedly suck away our hard-earned cash? Never. Halfway there, I had a choice: jump on a wide-open toll road or sit in a sea of traffic, only to arrive at my appointment swearing and frustrated. It was an easy but costly decision: My $6.50 toll quickly turned into a $70 fine. Apparently, the State of California decided to remove all the toll collection booths, claiming it was a move to save taxpayers' money. I think it was a trap designed to help them rake in more cash, luring unsuspecting drivers like me into paying over 10 times the standard rate.

Even the savviest person can get caught in a web of money traps. And the opportunity cost of ignoring these hidden wastes can add up to thousands of dollars—money that could be better spent building your net worth. The following are five common money traps lurking in our daily lives. But be aware: Businesses are constantly refining and creating new tricks of the trade designed to drain your wallet.

The "Free" Trial Offer

They say the best things in life are free. Not always. Ever wonder why businesses are willing to offer that free trial? Sure, it builds customer loyalty, and hopefully, you happily become a repeat buyer. However, companies also know that many of us never read the fine print, and they make no attempt to remind us when the free period is over. Instead, your "free" subscription or service converts to a paid one. And while they now have a steady revenue stream, you're left with an unwanted monthly expense. Your loss is their gain. Because credit cards are often used over debit cards to secure these offers, the average 22 percent APR of interest you're paying each year amounts to an even greater loss to your bottom line.

And here's where the trickiest trap hides: Many companies make it virtually impossible for you to cancel these offers, so that simple one-second click takes hours of phone calls and emails to undo. They are making a calculated bet that you'll get frustrated and give up—but that's something you simply can't afford to do. How do you avoid this trap? Say *no*! But if you can't resist a freebie, don't skip the fine print. You need to know exactly what you are agreeing to, mark your calendar when the trial ends, and most importantly, have an exit strategy so you can get out. Additionally, watch out for prechecked boxes. Often a single check-mark gives a company the right to extend their offer beyond the trial period, thus authorizing them to charge you. Ultimately, this gives you little recourse if you choose to later contest the charges. This is a real-life example of the benefits of your money date. That simple ritual will catch these types of reoccurring surprises early and save you money.

Spending to Save

Just because you have a coupon or the opportunity to take advantage of a great deal doesn't mean you need to act on it—especially if the bargain is for something you would not otherwise purchase, like a gallon of coconut oil or two dozen cinnamon buns. Recent studies show that 38 percent of us spend more because of a coupon, and 67 percent will purchase something we never intended to buy at all.[33] This tendency to spend to save, rather than to satisfy a genuine need, can quickly sabotage your 45-20-35 framework.

Warehouse membership stores such as Costco and Sam's Club are designed to make a saver out of you. Everything from their product placement, revolving door of new merchandise, and wide selection of tempting tasters is done to encourage spending. And it's working! Because the only way to spend less than $100 at Costco is to simply leave your wallet at home. While purchasing items in bulk has its advantages, be strategic. It's hard to imagine what a family of four is going to do with 2,250 Q-tips or 128 servings of salad dressing.

How do you avoid this trap? Steer clear of the center aisles and beware of special promotions—especially those at the end of aisles, known in the industry as end caps. Often, these end-cap items aren't even on sale; they are just higher-margin products merchandised to catch the shopper's eye. Be a buyer, not a shopper. Stick to a list and allot yourself a set amount of time, preferably at the end of the day when you are tired and less likely to meander through the aisles. Use the tasters to fill your stomach, not your cart. Just another reason to carry cash—having limited resources means making limited purchases.

The Upsell

You're standing at the rental car counter after a hellish day of airline travel only to be bombarded by a slew of questions: How about we upgrade you to a convertible? Would you like to prepurchase a tank of gas? Need additional insurance coverage? What about a GPS? (As you hold your smartphone.) And the one that always puzzles me the most given the ages of my kids: Do you need a car seat?

"No, no, no, no, and no!" Nice try.

These money traps are designed to make the company richer and you poorer. Upselling is a technique whereby a seller entices a buyer to purchase additional items to make a more profitable sale. Rental car companies aren't the only culprits. Retailers, technology companies, consumer electronic stores, and car dealerships offering extended warranties and after-market products regularly employ this tactic. Hell, even McDonald's has mastered the upsell with its supersize offers—and that doesn't just affect your wallet but your waistline, too!

How do you avoid this trap?

Do your homework and ask questions. Know what you already own so you don't make a redundant purchase. For example, only 10 percent of consumers need to purchase additional rental car insurance, yet more than 60 percent elect to pay a daily rate that is almost as much as the rental car itself. Before deciding on a warranty, you need to consider the reliability of the product you are purchasing and understand what the manufacturer is already offering. Many of us skip analyzing the economics—like the warranty fee as a percentage of sale price, the average non-warranty repair cost, any potential deductible, and the product's expected life cycle. Also, consider the actual probability of something breaking—often we act solely on the fear of what could happen.

And when you do say no, stick to it. Don't let the power of persuasion take you down. Some sellers use fear tactics to make you think you can't afford not to have these add-on items. Truth is, most of the time you can't afford to buy them.

The Pink Tax

A 2015 study titled "From Cradle to Cane: The Cost of Being a Female Consumer" by the NYC Department of Consumer and Worker Protection (formerly the Department of Consumer Affairs) found that products designed for women cost up to 13 percent more than the same items marketed to men. This price disparity is the result of the pink tax, which affects everything from personal care products and clothing to haircuts and even dry cleaning. Although it's not an actual government tax, the pink tax refers to inflated prices on goods and services marketed to women, with similar, lower-cost options available for men, creating a potential money trap. Over time, this hidden cost can add up, causing women to pay, on average, an extra $1,300 each year.[34]

Avoiding this trap can be tricky, but with some awareness and strategic thinking, you can minimize its impact on your wallet. Start by opting for unisex versions of certain products like razors, vitamins, body lotions, and soaps. Consider sticking to generic or store brands, which can save you up to 30 percent on the same goods. And if you simply must have that product from your favorite skin care line, wait for a sale and stock up.

Behavioral Target Marketing

Imagine binge watching *Fixer Upper* on your iPad until the wee hours of the morning only to wake up a few hours later to an ad from Floor & Decor, Magnolia Home, or Home Depot. Well, it's not a coincidence. This is called behavioral target marketing, and it is a serious money trap. Targeted ads pop up for products that match to your recent digital activity—even sometimes from the words you text or speak into your phone. And this makes it far too easy for you to click to buy something you never intended.

Pretty unsettling, huh?

To avoid falling into this trap, adjust your privacy settings on social media or other online accounts to minimize data sharing, limit cookies by disabling them in your browser settings, clear your browsing data regularly, and explore using alternative web browsers that prioritize your privacy, like DuckDuckGo. For those ads that still pop up, try the 7-Day Rule challenge: If you can't shake the temptation after a week, it might just be something worth considering.

Of course, not all technology is designed to drain your wallet; some tools are actually meant to help you save. Coupon apps, cash-back apps, and price comparison apps are great resources. However, to truly benefit from them, you need to know how to use them effectively—and, most importantly, only for what you actually need. If you're smartphone challenged like me, that's no easy task. Even as a savvy shopper, I often find myself using only coupons that I can physically grab from a display. When I see a bar code instead, I typically just toss the item in my cart and move on rather than risk another frustrating attempt at setting up yet one more app. And that's about as wasteful as tossing a $20 bill out the window of my car.

If you too find yourself struggling with this digital divide, take the time to ask for help. Approach a nearby employee or visit the service desk. And when all else fails, ask your kids—or maybe even your four-year-old grandchild! It blows my mind how quickly little kids grasp these things—and how often they end up teaching *us* something.

• • •

Bottom line: While understanding your vision and creating a plan is an essential step toward financial freedom and living a meaningful and authentic life, incorporating that plan into your daily routine is where real progress happens. It's easy to set goals. But it takes consistency and awareness to turn those goals into reality.

Throughout this chapter, we've explored practical strategies and best practices to help you not only stay on track but also build the money habits that make financial success sustainable. By incorporating these practices into your daily routine, you'll begin to see momentum—and as that momentum grows, so will your confidence in making wiser, more strategic decisions with your money.

It's important to remember that it takes time to form new habits, so be patient with yourself. Commit to practicing these actions daily, stay consistent, and above all, keep repeating—because persistence is the key to turning your plan into lasting success.

Chapter Nine

Step Six—Build Your Team

> *Teamwork makes the dream work.*
> —John C. Maxwell,
> *Teamwork Makes the Dream Work*

E ven after all the work I had done to build a solid financial foundation for the next chapter of my life, it didn't take long for me to
realize I still needed help. Within months of being on my own, I had
become much more strategic in my overall approach to money, but there
was still *a lot* I didn't know—what stocks to buy, how best to incorporate
bonds into the mix, who should handle my taxes, and how to protect the
boys if I were to die (uncomfortable to think about, I know, but a critical
issue I couldn't ignore).

It became quite clear that managing all the aspects of my wealth
wasn't a DIY job. It would require experts, and there's no one-size-fits-all
solution—not for me or for you. Each one of us is unique, with different

goals to accomplish, varying amounts of money to manage, and specific issues to address. These factors and more should be considered when determining the kind of advice you need.

For some of us, web-based tools like personal finance apps, robo-advisors, online legal services, and tax software are great resources to consider. Virtual and in-person female-focused communities can also provide valuable financial education and planning tools. Others might require personal experts, including an investment advisor, a CPA, or an estate planning attorney. Whatever their roles, these experts should be someone you can trust and who have your (and only your) best interest at heart. They should talk *with* you, not *at* you; communicate in plain language; encourage you to ask questions; and remain committed to helping you learn.

Knowing when and how to find these advisors isn't necessarily easy. Without the right know-how, you could end up in the wrong hands, wasting both time and money—or possibly worse! Throughout this chapter, I share insights to help you determine which advisors you might need, who's best equipped to help, the questions to ask before hiring them, and the pitfalls to watch out for. Regardless of your circumstance, surrounding yourself with the right resources and support is essential—and it often starts with a trustworthy financial advisor.

Your Financial Advisor

While you might have a good understanding of what a CPA or an estate planning attorney does, recognizing who's who in the world of financial advice can get tricky. It's important to keep in mind that the term *financial advisor* is a generic term under which all types of financial advisors fall, including those that aren't human.

In 2008, the financial services industry saw the rise of a new innovation: the robo-advisor. While not a physical robot, this automated platform uses algorithms to deliver financial planning and investment services. And although this deviates from traditional financial advisory that emphasizes personal relationships, it offers some good benefits, including lower fees (up to 75 percent less than traditional advisors) and greater accessibility—especially for those just starting out or with limited assets to manage. But to me, nothing outweighs the value of human connection. I generally recommend working with a real-life advisor if possible—someone you can build a lasting relationship with and who can be there to address your evolving needs because they will inevitably change over time.

There are a lot of different options out there, so before deciding which one is right for you, it's important to understand a few key definitions.

Broker: A broker acts as an intermediary who buys and sells securities* on your behalf. Typically, their work is transaction based rather than relationship based. There are two main types of brokerage firms: discount brokers (e.g., E*Trade, Robinhood, TD Ameritrade) and full-service brokers (e.g., Merrill Lynch, Charles Schwab, Fidelity Investments).

While discount brokers just execute trades and don't provide any other services or types of advice, full-service firms—also known as wirehouses—have large research departments that provide detailed reports and investment recommendations to clients. Many of these firms also have investment banking divisions that help corporations and governments raise capital, sell or buy businesses, or manage risks. These firms typically offer some of their clients access to exclusive financial

---

* Securities are financial assets you can easily buy, sell, or trade—like a stock, bond, mutual fund, or ETF. Think of them as investment tools to help grow your money over time.

products, like initial public offerings (IPOs),* as well as in-house products like mutual funds,† exchange-trades funds (ETFs),‡ loan service, and insurance.

Financial planner: A financial planner is a professional who helps you take a good look at your current finances and works with you to create a savings, investing, and retirement plan that aligns with both your short-term and long-term goals. Sometimes financial planners work independently and offer only planning advice, while others are part of larger teams at full-service brokerage houses, banks, insurance companies, or wealth management firms. In many cases, financial planners may also serve as investment advisors, wealth managers, or brokers. However, it's important to note that not all brokers or wealth managers are financial planners.

Investment advisor: This type of advisor is someone who gives you investment recommendations and, with your consent, can also manage your investments on your behalf. If an investment advisor manages $100 million or more in total client assets, they have to register with the Securities and Exchange Commission (SEC) and are called registered investment advisors (RIAs). RIAs must avoid conflicts of interest. All recommendations need to align with their clients' needs and financial

---

* IPO stands for initial public offering. It occurs when a private company sells shares of its stock to the public for the first time, allowing anyone to buy and sell them on the stock market.

† A mutual fund is a pool of money collected from investors to buy a mix of stock, bonds, and other investments. Instead of picking these types of securities yourself, you invest in the fund and professional managers handle everything else. These funds are traded on the exchange once a day.

‡ An ETF is an exchange-traded fund. It is a basket of investments (like stocks and bonds) that you can buy and sell on the stock market. It's similar to a mutual fund, but ETFs are traded on the exchange all day long rather than just once a day.

circumstance, and their clients' transactions must always take priority over their own.

Wealth manager: These institutions generally focus on high-net-worth clients and often have some pretty substantial minimum investable asset requirements, which can vary from firm to firm. A wealth manager, also known as a private wealth manager, provides comprehensive financial services, including financial advice, financial planning, and investment management. They consider all aspects of a person's financial life, as well as their unique needs, to create both short-term and long-term solutions. Because a wealth advisor typically has a bird's-eye view of your entire financial picture, they often serve as the quarterback of your team and collaborate with your outside advisors to ensure you have a comprehensive plan in place.

See how it can get confusing?

To complicate things further, financial advisors often wear different hats at different times, making it challenging for you to understand their exact role and expertise. For instance, a broker can serve as a financial planner, but their primary responsibility is to buy and sell different types of securities rather than provide comprehensive financial planning and retirement advice. Additionally, an RIA may refer to itself as a wealth manager, or a wealth management firm can operate as a division within a larger financial institution that also includes a broker-dealer.

So how can you tell one type of advisor from another and confidently know what type is right for you? First and foremost, it's critical you understand how each is paid, which typically falls under four categories—commission, fee only, fee based, or flat fee.

Commission: Commission-based advisors earn fees from selling products. And while there's technically nothing wrong with this payment structure, I am a bit skeptical working with anyone compensated this way. Right out of the gate, I am worried that these advisors might try to sell me something I don't truly need, which means that my best interests don't come before theirs.

Fee only: One the other hand, fee-only advisors charge a fee based on the total assets they manage for you. While this payment structure might sound ideal—since they earn more as you earn more—it depends on the rate they charge, which often starts at about 1 percent. If the fee becomes too high relative to the services you need, this can become a significant concern. Additionally, most fee-only advisors have a minimum amount they're willing to manage, which means you might need to have a few hundred thousand dollars—even more—before they want to work with you.

Fee based: Fee-based advisors typically use a hybrid approach, charging a percentage on the total assets they manage while also earning commissions on the products they recommend—again creating a potential conflict of interest.

Flat fee: Advisors that charge a flat fee often do so to create a financial plan but leave the investing to you.

Next, it's essential that you take the time to understand their lingo and credentials. This was my blind side. As I began talking with prospective financial advisors, they started throwing out one acronym after another—CFA, CPA, RIA—along with terms like fiduciary, registered rep, and custodian. I felt a lot like Charlie Brown trying to understand an adult in the *Peanuts* cartoon. All I heard was "wah, wah, wah," leaving me totally confused. And to make matters worse, the people across the table from me jumped to some big conclusions about what I knew. Since I had been in private equity, they were sure I understood exactly what they were talking about.

Well, I didn't.

Finance is a lot like medicine. There's a big difference between a heart surgeon and an OB-GYN. I wouldn't want the former performing a C-section on me, just as I wouldn't want the latter unclogging my arteries. Just because I knew what EBITDA (earnings before interest, tax, depreciation, and amortization) meant or understood the difference between pre-money and post-money valuation didn't mean I had any idea what RIA stood for, what it meant when they said they were a fiduciary, and how they differed from the next guy.

The entire experience made me want to crawl into a hole. I felt small—stupid in many ways. It wasn't until one day when a good friend—a former engineer at Qualcomm and now owner of several businesses (and a man, I should add)—looked at one of those same financial advisors and said, "What in the hell is an RIA?" that I realized this was their issue—not mine. But it was my problem that I didn't have the courage to stop them like he did—to speak up and call them out on their jargon.

Shame on me!

As women we must stop feeling ashamed or embarrassed about our situation. Instead, we need to own it and change it. There is no shame in what you don't know; shame lies in what you don't take on to learn. Think about that as you're talking with your prospective advisors. Don't allow it to be a one-sided conversation, and most importantly, make sure they speak to you in plain language.

When you ask them about their credentials—dive deep! Learn what the letters behind their name mean in terms of their specialty and what it took to earn them. Take a Chartered Financial Analyst (CFA) as an example. In many ways, these people are the rock stars of the investment management industry. To become one, you must have a bachelor's degree, accumulate 4,000 hours of relevant work experience over at least three consecutive years, and pass three six-hour exams that are notoriously challenging and often require 900 hours or more of study. That's why less than 20 percent of those who attempt the program ultimately earn the credential. A Certified Financial Planner (CFP) is another widely respected credential and is considered the gold standard in financial planning, as opposed to investing. Candidates must meet education requirements, complete extensive training, pass a six-hour exam, and adhere to certain ethical standards that prioritizes their clients' interests. But you won't know this type of stuff unless you dig in.

When it comes to industry lingo, there is a lot to keep track of, but the most crucial term you need to know is *fiduciary*. A fiduciary is a person or organization that is legally—and ethically—obligated to act in your best interest rather than their own. But watch out—not all financial advisors are fiduciaries. There is a big difference between someone who claims to "act as a fiduciary" and someone who actually is one. For example, a broker may claim they always put their clients' interests first, and maybe they genuinely do. However, brokers are not legally bound by a fiduciary duty and may recommend investments or products that generate higher commissions for themselves—even if those options aren't necessarily the best for their clients.

The bottom line: First, take time to create a short list of prospective financial advisors. Seek referrals from friends, family, colleagues, or other advisors you might be working with. If you choose to use an online resource to help generate your list, be aware that they may receive referral fees from the advisors, which can create an inherent bias. And if you're just not sure you can afford to hire anyone at this time, a wonderful resource to check out is Savvy Ladies, a nonprofit organization that offers free financial education to all women. Next, do your homework. Ask your potential advisor the right questions to ensure you find the ideal fit for you. These might include:

* Are you legally obligated as a fiduciary?
* How are you paid, both you and your firm?

* Is there anything that you get financially incentivized to do? For example: If you suggest a solution for me, such as insurance, are you getting paid something if I purchase it?
* What services or products does your firm offer?
* What's your client-to-advisor ratio?
* What is your (and your firm's) client retention rate?
* How will you invest my money? Do you invest in stocks, or do you select specific products or fund managers?
* Where will my assets be held?
* What are your credentials?
* How long have you been with your firm? What does the firm's turnover look like?
* Who would be part of my team? Does your firm have additional experts in case I need them, such as insurance, lending, financial education, etc.

Then ask yourself:

* Are these folks listening to me and really taking the time to understand my needs?
* Are they asking me insightful questions that show me they work with people like me?
* Are they throwing around a lot of jargon, or are they speaking in plain language?
* Are they making things confusing, or are they explaining things in a way that I can understand and gives me confidence to ask more questions?
* Do I feel like I will get the attention I need, or am I just a small fish in a big pond to them?

You can also research an advisor's background by visiting https://adviserinfo.sec.gov and looking up their Form ADV, which all registered advisors must file with the SEC. This will detail the services they offer, investment philosophy, background and qualifications, as well as the types of clients the advisor typically works with. Additionally, check out BrokerCheck, a website of the Financial Industry Regulatory Authority (FINRA). Here you can review each individual's employment record and check for red flags, including disciplinary actions.

Whatever you do, don't rush. Talk to multiple folks (at least three). This is your money, and in many ways, your relationship with your financial advisor is like a marriage—they're going to know a lot about you! You'd never say yes to a proposal on the first date, would you? Why should this be any different? So don't let anyone pressure you into making a decision before you are ready. At the end of the day, there is no perfect solution for every situation. It's all about knowing your blind side, educating yourself, understanding your risks, and doing all that you can to ensure you are working with someone you trust.

Your Tax Advisor

Now let's talk about a topic you should rarely (if ever) tackle on your own: taxes. When it comes to knowing where to turn for help, it's important to start with the end in mind, because not all tax experts are created equal. Some only prepare taxes, others provide only tax advice, and some do both.

For individuals with simple returns—such as income from one source like W-2 wages, a standard IRS deduction, and maybe a limited number of tax credits or adjustments—tax preparation firms, such as H&R Block and Jackson Hewitt, or online platforms, such as TurboTax or TaxAct, might be a good fit. While these low-cost solutions may do fine work, they lack the personal relationship that's essential for someone with complex finances or those seeking ongoing tax advice, including strategies to reduce what they owe each year to Uncle Sam.

It's also important to know that *only* Certified Public Accounts (CPAs), Enrolled Agents (a federally licensed tax practitioner), and tax attorneys can represent you before the IRS. In other words, everyone else can only tell you what you owe in taxes, and if the IRS doesn't think that number is right, you'll have to defend yourself in an audit. That's not something I'd wish upon anyone! These tax professionals are held to a higher standard of education and expertise, which is why I generally recommend them over someone who is less credentialed. In fact, leading experts assert that uncredentialed tax preparers pose a significant risk to taxpayers, often using the filing process to market expensive products or, in some cases, to steal personal information for identity theft.

Once you've narrowed down what you need, you can start searching for referrals. But before you turn to Google, begin with your personal network. Ask friends, family, and colleagues, especially those in a situation similar to yours, for recommendations. If you own a small business, for example, ask another small business owner who they use, how long they've been working together, and what specific services they provide. More often than not, business owners need ongoing advice to ensure they are optimizing the deductions they are entitled to.

You can also turn to professional organizations like the National Association of Enrolled Agents (NAEA) or the American Institute of Certified Public Accountants (AICPA), as well as the IRS's online directory, for a list of qualified advisors in your area. It's worth noting that if you make less than $64,000 or are a person with a disability, you may qualify for free tax preparation services through the IRS's Volunteer Income Tax Assistance (VITA) program. Do your homework. Check online reviews and schedule time to talk with each professional. Ask them questions like:

* What credentials do you have?
* How long have you been in business?

* Do you have a specific area of expertise?
* Who are your typical clients?
* What other services do you, or your firm, offer?
* How many families are you currently working with?
* Who will be doing the work? And how accessible are you?
* Can you represent me if I am audited?
* If needed, are you willing to work with my other advisors, such as my financial adviser or my estate planning attorney?
* How will you charge me?

For an average tax return, you can expect to pay between $250 and $300, depending on whether you take the standard deduction or choose to itemize. Tax preparers charge in different ways: by the hour, with a minimum fee plus costs based on the complexity of your return, or a set fee for each form and schedule needed. If you encounter a tax preparer who bases their fee on the size of your refund or who promises a bigger refund than other preparers, that's a big red flag.

And that's not the only warning sign to watch out for. Paid preparers are required by law to have a Preparer Tax Identification Number (PTIN) and to sign their clients' returns. If you find yourself speaking with someone who doesn't comply with either requirement, it's a good idea to walk away. The IRS also mandates that anyone who prepares more than 11 returns each year for clients must file electronically. So, if a preparer doesn't offer e-filing as an option, they may not be as experienced as you thought. And never sign a blank return—doing so allows the preparer to add anything they want, including their own bank account number, which could lead to them stealing your refund.

It's also worth sharing that most tax software providers offer a free version of their programs, but before you take advantage of one, be sure to read the fine print. In most cases, you can bet there's a catch—such as limited features or hidden fees and upsells.

Your Estate Planning Advisor

A few months back, my aunt called. Her voice was filled with anxiety. She's 78, and I am her only surviving relative. "Steph, I was at the bank today, and Judy"—her banker for the last 20 years—"is really worried about what will happen to my accounts when I die."

"Aunt Leslie, do you have a will?" I asked, my heart sinking.

"No," she replied.

As our conversation continued, I learned that she didn't have *any* estate planning documents in place. No will, no medical directive, no powers of attorney—nothing that would allow me to communicate with her doctors or make decisions on her behalf if she ever became incapacitated. Nothing that would grant me the authority to ensure her bills were paid. Nothing to make the already daunting task of navigating the hell of estate settlement—this bureaucratic labyrinth—any easier. Ugh!

"Do you love me?" I pressed.

"Of course I do," she responded, a bit puzzled by my question. "I'll be dead, and none of this will matter."

"Yes, but I won't be," I shot back.

According to Caring.com's 2024 Wills Survey, nearly 70 percent of Americans are in the same boat as my aunt, which also means their loved ones are likely facing the same reality I am. Far too many people neglect this type of essential planning, thinking it's too complicated, too expensive, or only for the wealthy. Well, none of that is true, and not doing it can leave your family members facing a logistical and financial headache. Without a will, intestate laws take over. This means that when you die, all your assets will be frozen, and the court system will sift through every detail and decide how what you own gets divvied up—potentially giving your hard-earned money to that family member you haven't spoken to in over two decades.

The ramification of not having the proper documents in place extends far beyond your money. Have you ever heard of Terri Schiavo's story? She was the Florida woman who, at just 26, was left in a vegetative state after going into cardiac arrest. Because her wishes were not known and no one had the legal authority to make decisions on her behalf, a legal battle ensued.[35] Terri's situation divided her family because her husband and parents emphatically disagreed over her medical care. This led to a 15-year legal battle and divisive national debate. In another tragic case, a young couple died in a car accident, leaving behind two young daughters. Because they didn't have a will, the decision of who would raise the children fell to the court. And ultimately, the little girls were placed with relatives they hardly knew instead of with their parents' close friends who had always been considered family.

One simple document could have prevented each of these nightmares. To protect your family, yourself, and your wealth, at minimum you'll need a will (with guardianship directives if needed), a durable power of attorney, a health care power of attorney, and a medical directive, also known as a living will. In case you are unfamiliar with any of these terms, here are some basic definitions.

* **Guardianship Directive:** A legal document that designates who will take care of your children if something happened to you before they turn 18.
* **Durable Power of Attorney:** A legal document that names someone you trust to make financial decisions and handle important matters if you become sick, injured, or unable to do so yourself. This person can help with paying bills, managing bank accounts and investments, and handling your real estate or business affairs.
* **Medical Directive:** A legal document that outlines your medical treatment wishes in advance, in case you ever become too sick or injured to communicate them yourself.

* **Health Care Power of Attorney:** A legal document that appoints someone to make medical decisions for you if you should become incapacitated. This person can approve or refuse medical treatments, make decisions about medications or surgeries, choose doctors and health care facilities, and follow your wishes about life support or end-of-life care.

Additionally, be sure to review all the beneficiary designations—specifically, the names listed on your 401(k), IRAs, life insurance, and HSAs. These individuals will receive the funds in these accounts if something happens to you. Keep in mind that beneficiary designations generally override what's specified in your will. In fact, one of the biggest mistakes people make after divorce is forgetting to update these designations—potentially resulting in your ex inheriting these accounts after you pass away. And that's definitely not ideal!

Don't think this stuff is just for you: Anyone over 18 should prepare most of these documents. Although your 18-year-old who is off enjoying his freshman year at college might have only $10 to his name, if he's injured and winds up in the hospital, you won't have access to his medical information or the ability to make health care decisions on his behalf without his consent. That's unsettling!

When it comes to creating your estate plan, there are several options, depending on your situation. For straightforward cases—where your assets are modest and you know exactly who you want to care for your kids and inherit your assets—online resources like Trust & Will, Good-Trust, LegalZoom, and Quicken's WillMaker can be excellent solutions. And as you evaluate each option, keep the following in mind:

* **User friendliness:** Ensure the platform is easy to navigate and has good customer service.
* **Data security:** Look for strong encryption and a privacy protocol that will protect your personal information.

* **Pricing structure:** Do they charge a subscription fee, a one-time flat fee, or a fee based on the number of documents you request?
* **Legal compliance:** Be certain their documents comply with your state's laws and check to see if you can request access to an attorney if needed.

For larger and more complex estates—such as those involving trusts, childcare concerns, complex assets, or nonfamily beneficiaries—it's important that you seek out an attorney. The same applies if you have questions about the estate settlement process or you're simply not comfortable managing all this on your own. In fact, even if you choose to use an online platform, I suggest consulting with a professional to confirm you haven't overlooked anything or inadvertently taken steps that don't align with your intentions.

Start with your network. Turn to your other advisors—as well as your family members, friends, and colleagues—and ask them for referrals. Then check these attorneys out! Consider researching their lawyer ratings on third-party verified sites like Martindale-Hubbell or Avvo. These platforms do not charge attorneys to be listed and have created their own criteria for ratings, both of which helps to ensure a more objective assessment. In fact, I'd avoid regular online directories all together. Most are only filled with attorneys who pay to be included on the list. Once you have a short list of candidates, spend some time with each attorney. Ask them questions like:

* Is your primary focus on estate planning?
* Where did you go to law school?
* What credentials do you have? What do those credentials mean, and what did it take to earn them?
* What does your typical client look like?
* How long have you worked with your average client/family?
* What's your process?
* Do you have a formal updating and maintenance program?

* What other services do you offer?
* How do you charge? Flat fee? Hourly?
* Do you carry malpractice insurance?
* What organizations do you belong to?

The benchmark for excellence in estate planning is the American College of Trust and Estate Counsel (ACTEC). Membership is highly exclusive, available by invitation only, and solely based on nominations from other ACTEC fellows. So, if one of the attorneys you're considering is a member of ACTEC, you can rest assured they're among the best of the best. However, keep in mind there are only 2,400 fellows across the United States, so don't make membership your only criteria. There are plenty of great ones out there who are not part of ACTEC.

It's also worth noting that the average hourly rate for an estate planning attorney ranges from $250 to $310, while flat fee packages can range from $750 to well over $5,000, depending on your needs. The good news is that most attorneys offer a free initial consultation, so I highly suggest that you take advantage of this opportunity. Asking questions and gathering information will help you feel more confident in identifying the right fit for you.

Your Community

One of the best ways to complement your team of experts is by joining a female-focused community where you can connect with other women, share successes, navigate challenges, and learn from each other. These networks provide financial education, peer support, and expert insight—all of which are key to your long-term success.

You can find these groups through online platforms, social media groups, local organizations, or financial institutions such as banks and investment firms that offer curated financial literacy programs, expert guidance, and opportunities to build meaningful relationships—all of which empower confident financial decision-making. By embracing a trusted community, you can feel more supported and informed as you navigate your financial journey.

Your Role with Your Team

When it comes to your financial team, you are without a doubt the most important member. No one knows your goals, dreams, and values better than you. While your financial advisor, tax professional, and attorney can provide valuable support, it's your vision and unique needs that guide them and ultimately shape your plans.

My top piece of advice: Stay engaged. Regularly share your goals, concerns, and any changes in your personal or financial situation with your team. Communicate openly with each member as needed. Take the initiative to continually expand your knowledge of financial concepts, understand the reasoning behind their recommendations, and be aware of tax implications. This will help you know key questions to ask and make informed, confident decisions. And always, always, *speak up!* If you don't understand something—whether it's what someone said, the why behind their advice, or even the fees you're expected to pay—don't hesitate to ask! Remember, there's no shame in not knowing something. The only mistake is not taking advantage of those moments to lean in and learn.

Chapter Ten

Step Seven—Get Smart with Your Love Life

> *Fill up your cup and let them fall*
> *in love with the overflow.*
> —Unknown

One of the most surprising aspects of my journey has been how my newfound financial autonomy has illuminated new and much-needed perspectives on love, partnerships, and marriage. When I think back to that fateful night and reflect on my emotional reaction—along with everything I've learned about myself since—I can't help but wonder: Did I fight so hard after learning about Richard's affair, compromising my values and self-worth and putting myself through months of utter hell, because I truly loved Richard, felt a deep obligation to honor my vows, and wanted to keep our family intact for the sake of our sons? Or was much of it rooted in fear? Fear of losing the life I had and the comforts and stability that came with it, fear of letting go of the safe and familiar, fear of judgment and the social consequences of divorce, fear of stepping into the unknown, and fear around how to gain what I had lost all those years earlier?

Today I can say with 100 percent certainty that it was the latter.

No one wakes up one morning and decides, "I think I'll lose my financial independence today." For some, that independence never gets established in the first place; for others, it slips away gradually—whether consciously or unconsciously. Regardless of the situation, far too many of us fail to recognize the value of what we've lost and the risks we've exposed ourselves and our families to until life forces us to confront it.

I certainly didn't.

While divorce was my wake-up call, there are other circumstances that can put you at risk when you lack earning power, financial literacy, and a voice in financial decision-making. Consider women's longevity: Our average life expectancy is currently 81,[36] and it can extend by another 10 years or more with a healthy lifestyle.[37] Notably, 78 percent of those aged 100 or older are women, and that number is projected to quadruple over the next 30 years.[38] Moreover, 36 percent of all divorces today involve someone over 50.[39] At the same time, nearly one million women face widowhood each year at an average age of 59. In fact, half of all widows will outlive their husbands by an average of 12.5 years.[40]

All of this leads to one crucial conclusion: 8 out of 10 of us will be forced to navigate our financial lives alone. And unfortunately, far too many women will not be prepared to do so effectively because of the way we handled money during our marriage or partnership.

Marriage and Partnerships

When I rashly decided to quit my job, I believed it was what I needed to do to give our sons the childhood that Richard and I never had. I also knew that the growing demands of my career weren't sustainable and that something had to give. But not once did I stop to think about the opportunity cost of this decision. I simply believed it was *my* responsibility—as a wife and mother—to fix the problem on my own for the benefit of our family.

Richard supported my choice, but the decision was entirely mine.

I had been socialized to believe that being a "good woman" meant self-sacrifice—that putting aside my own needs and dreams for the sake of my family was an act of love for my children and my spouse. However, as a result of my journey and the countless stories I've heard from women across the country in my work, I now understand that this act of love carries substantial risk: It not only jeopardizes our ability to financially protect ourselves and our children, but it also often leads us to lose sight of who we are as individuals—our interests, personal desires, and professional aspirations. All of this is important for us and our families.

But this isn't just about our goals and the ability to earn; it's equally about our understanding of our money. As life became busier, the demands of running a household and raising children led to a division of duties between my husband and me. This caused me to voluntarily turn a blind eye to all financial matters. I stopped paying attention to the bills we owed, our checking account balances, and the debt we carried. I signed tax returns year after year without reading them and put my John Hancock on estate planning documents without having a clue to what I was agreeing to. And just like my mother, I was content to receive my "weekly allowance."

I take complete responsibility for all this, too.

At times, we can also unconsciously lose some of our agency, revealing the subtle dynamics of gender power within a marriage. I remember several moments as a stay-at-home mom when Richard would say, "I just can't keep up with you," implying that I was somehow emasculating him. Frankly, I wasn't quite sure how, since I didn't even have a job—he was the one with the impressive career that had him jet-setting all over the country and earning well into six figures. In response, I took this on as my problem, when really it was his. I subconsciously throttled back my energy and expressed more gratitude for everything he was doing to enable me to stay home with the kids. I boosted his ego at every opportunity, even if it meant sacrificing my own sense of self in the process.

It's easy to get caught in a spider web woven over the years. Each individual filament might not be strong enough to trap you, but collectively—if there are enough of them—you may awaken one day to find that you've been pinned down and immobilized, leaving you with little to no ability to change course. Considering the realities women face today—especially the impact of our longer lifespans—we simply can't afford to let this happen.

I wasn't the only one who suffered from my choices and actions. I now see how my eventual lack of economic agency took a toll on Richard and our marriage, too. I remember back in 2008—at the onset of the financial crisis—lying in bed as Richard tossed and turned, ultimately getting up at 4 a.m. nearly every day to walk the streets of our neighborhood, desperately trying to shake his anxiety. I didn't fully understand the weight on his shoulders as the markets were crashing, banks were closing, and homes were being foreclosed. His distress wasn't just because our retirement accounts were down nearly 40 percent. He worked for a financial institution and feared losing his job—our only source of income—which added yet another layer of fear to his already heavy burden.

While I was busy driving carpool, cooking, doing laundry, and shuttling the boys to practices and playdates, he was consumed by the instability of the economy and his ongoing ability to keep the wheels on the bus moving. I failed to recognize how I could support him, but frankly, not once did he stop and ask me for help.

Marriage is much more than a romantic partnership; it's also an emotional and financial one. Neither partner should shoulder the burden of a family's financial well-being alone. Instead, it should be a joint venture centered around this idea: "I am here for you; you are here for me."

In the 1950s, 65 percent of all children were raised in traditional breadwinner-homemaker families; today, that number is closer to 22 percent.[41] Yet New York Life's 2024 Wealth Watch survey showed that over 60 percent of married men claim they still make nearly all of their family's financial decisions, which can ultimately create pressures that can be intolerable—especially during tough times.

Some of the ways we have defined what it means to be a man, starting from childhood, imposes unrealistic and harmful standards. Boys are taught not to cry, to "buck up," and that showing weakness or failure is unacceptable. The societal pressure to adhere to ideals of strength, stoicism, and emotional control can make it incredibly difficult for a man to open up, be fully transparent about his fears, and ask for help. And while I deeply appreciate and admire the strong, confident man and his inherent desire to protect his wife, that shielding should never come at the expense of her ability to provide for herself and their children in the event something happens to him. Nor should it be at the expense of the man's own emotional well-being.

Instead, we must consider each other's needs, creating a space where all of us can be fully human—flawed, fallible, and honest about the challenges we're facing. As women, we should encourage our male partners to embrace their vulnerabilities without fear of shame and judgment. Because when men feel they must hold back their emotions to prove their worth, they risk losing touch with their sense of self.

Darwin never said that the strongest survive. Instead, his theory of evolution centers on the concept of natural selection—the idea that it is not the strongest or the most intelligent that survives, but those most adaptable to change. As our world has evolved over the past 50 years, so too must our views on the traditional roles within families. By allowing both men and women to express their authentic selves, we can build true partnerships where responsibilities—including financial ones—are more broadly shared within a marriage. This includes creating new money habits and behaviors, emphasizing greater financial transparency, and encouraging deep, meaningful conversations about money—during both good times and bad.

How do you put this into practice? Use your regular money date to foster intentional communication, recognize and play to each other's strengths, establish shared goals and "what-if" scenarios, and ensure transparency and an equal voice in the conversation.

Let's take a closer look at each.

Have Intentional Communication

What you say to each other is important, but even more critical is *how* you say it. Just as you have a money story, your partner has their own, shaped by life experiences that are likely very different from yours. To have ongoing, productive conversations about money, it's essential for both of you to take the time to understand each other's perspectives, triggers, and communication styles.

Talk openly about your childhood experiences, the money messages you each received, and the behaviors (good and bad) you've adapted because of your respective journeys. Then, openly discuss the differences and what you both need to do to meet the other where they're at to discuss financial issues.

Recognize and Play to Each Other's Strengths

Even if finance isn't your thing, it's important that both you and your partner stay involved in managing your household's financial responsibilities—even if one person ultimately takes the lead. Make it a priority to discuss what's needed, then consider each other's strengths and interests. For example, one of you might excel at navigating health care issues and insurance while the other might be more comfortable handling budgeting and taxes. By identifying your respective strengths, you can divide the financial tasks in a way that leverages each person's abilities. Along the way, take the opportunity to teach and support each other, building a mutual understanding and enhancing your financial partnership.

Establish Shared Goals and "What-If" Scenarios

Whether you want to buy a house, start a business, pay off debt, save for your kids' college, or build a travel fund for annual vacations, you and your partner need to be on the same page. While this might sound like an obvious best practice for couples, studies show that nearly 40 percent of partners don't—often leading to conflict over competing priories.[42] It's equally important to talk about the inevitable: those curveballs life throws our way that can derail even the best-laid plans. Discuss your family's monthly needs versus wants, and together, identify which expenses could be cut if times get tough. Having this conversation in advance can help you both feel more confident during stressful periods—and reduce the risk of arguments and panic when challenges arise.

Ensure Transparency and an Equal Voice

Studies show that 65 percent of couples admit to hiding purchases from their partner,[43] and far too many don't discuss major purchases at all. I certainly watched my mom stash packages in the trunk of her car only to pull them out days later when my dad wasn't around. Frankly, both behaviors are recipes for disaster because the only outcome is resentment.

Honesty and transparency are crucial in any relationship. Regardless of whether one person primarily manages the finances, both partners should stay engaged and informed. Have open discussions about important topics, like big purchases (planned or unplanned), savings goals, and potential financial challenges. Most importantly, listen to each other's thoughts and concerns. By fostering an open dialogue, you'll build a stronger sense of partnership and mutual respect around all money matters. Last, all of this should be modeled for our children so that we can encourage healthy partnerships around money for generations to come.

Single or Life After Marriage

Eventually, I did find love again. But it wasn't the traditional blueprint society tells us is the end goal, nor did my partner—or our relationship—resemble anything from my previous life. For over a decade, I was with an extraordinary man named Matt. We never married, and although we lived together, we spent a lot of time apart. We both deeply loved each other and were (and in many ways still are) wholeheartedly committed to one another, although now just as dear friends. We have each gone through pain and loss—he with cancer as well as divorce—and have had to rebuild our lives. When we met, Matt was just a few months into remission, still carrying the physical reminder of his battle with the port-a-cath implanted in his chest. We were both beaten down, emotionally drained from our respective struggles and desperately wanting to find ourselves again. We had completely different interests and skill sets. I may have been a builder of wealth, but he was a builder of things—initially a fireman, then a general contractor, restorer of classic cars, and my very own MacGyver. We also had entirely different want structures and financial means.

When Matt was diagnosed with an incurable form of cancer at the age of 50, he changed his life dramatically. The drive and ambition he once had to earn money transformed into a strong desire to simplify his life, preserve his wealth, and value experiences over anything material. If this meant driving a 15-year-old car or traveling to South America with just a backpack, so be it. At the same time, he always respected my ambition and understood my need to prioritize my earning power for the sake of my boys and my long-term financial security. He also knew that when I could afford it, I wanted to indulge a bit in some finer things.

Matt never tried to change me, and I never sought to change him. I didn't care about the money he had—or didn't have. I was determined to create my own. And as my wealth grew, he made it abundantly clear that he never wanted to be financially dependent on me—just as I never wanted to be dependent on him all those years earlier when I was still financially unstable.

Our independence extended far beyond our finances. We were also 12 years apart, which led to very different aspirations. Matt eventually was ready to check out and relax on a beach, while in many ways, I felt as though I was just getting started—professionally and personally. Despite our many differences, we always recognized the importance of supporting each other's personal growth and our respective dreams and desires, as well as ensuring that neither of us lost sight of who we worked so hard to become.

Our love was about compromise, not sacrifice. Matt and I rewrote the script that society told us what we needed to follow to live out our happily ever after—even if our time together wasn't forever. And it was pretty damn good, until the day we both realized that, despite our love for each other, our season together was over.

For those of you who are single, I am not suggesting that the path Matt and I took is right for everyone. Nor am I certain it's even what I want for my future. In fact, I recently met an incredible man, and for the first time in a long time, I'm starting to think I might want to get married again. Perhaps, I will; perhaps, I won't. I simply don't know.

What I am saying is that once you free yourself from outdated narratives—"I can't be happy alone," "I need a partner to feel complete," "My partner has to fit a certain mold," or "Marriage is the final goal for all solid loving relationships"—you might begin to see other possibilities that may bring you more joy, happiness, and self-discovery in that moment.

Matt and I were together because we *wanted* to be, not because we *needed* to be. Our relationship was on our own terms—and no one else's. This intentionality gave us both the space to truly understand who we were as individuals, what we each sought in a partnership, and what we had to give. Throughout this process, I've learned that true wholeness—that deep sense of self-acceptance and fulfillment—comes from within, not from anything you receive from someone or something else. Only you can make yourself complete; only you can find peace within your own skin. The power of unconditional love lies in *wanting* that person in your life, not in *needing* them—physically, emotionally, or financially—to survive. Love isn't about dependency. I had a man who never stood in my way. In fact, as my dreams got bigger—and my goals got even hairier—he just kept saying, "Fly, Steph, fly."

• • •

When Matt and I ended our relationship, I was heartbroken. But as I began to reflect on the foundation of our relationship—the love, the respect, and our independence—I recognized that this ending was, in fact, an act of love from each of us to the other, and in many ways, it was a new and necessary beginning for both of us.

We both came to realize that as our individual needs and desires began to shift, we were no longer aligned. At 65 and physically fit, Matt felt a strong pull to see and experience the world while he still could. He understood that I wasn't in the same place in life. I still have a long list of goals—publishing this book, for one—and there are many more things I want to accomplish before I'm ready to slow down.

Staying together would eventually mean one of us sacrificing our path—and likely lead to resentment. Matt didn't want to hold me back from my goals, and I certainly didn't want to hold him back from his. For that, I am deeply grateful we both had the wisdom to recognize it—and the maturity and courage to honor it.

While it took months to move past the pain, what surprised me the most was how different this breakup was from the one I experienced with Richard. Yes, I was devastated. My eyes were just as swollen from all the crying, and I endured sleepless nights for weeks. But beyond not needing to worry about the impact this separation would have on young children—now that all three of my boys were in their 20s—the most significant difference between this relationship ending and the end of my marriage years earlier was this: Not once did I worry about how this would affect me financially, where I would live, or how I would survive.

Fear was no longer part of my emotional landscape. Instead, I felt a deep sense of trust in myself. I knew I could move forward and embrace the unknown.

The reason behind that was my financial independence—a gift I had committed to giving myself all those years earlier. In many ways, it felt like a full-circle moment—a realization that I was no longer the same person I was in my past relationship and that version of me was gone forever. I will forever be grateful to Matt. Our time together taught me so much about myself and the true meaning of love—not just with him, but, most importantly, with myself. I wouldn't be who I am or where I am in my life without him. Nor would I be able to love the way I do—or be the partner I am today, in my new relationship—without all of those experiences.

I believe that the people who enter and exit your life do so for many reasons, and it's important to recognize and honor the seasons they represent. Every relationship—whether romantic or otherwise, lasting years or just a moment—brings valuable experiences and lessons that contribute to your personal growth and prepare you for the next phase of your journey.

Conclusion

My journey has taught me how quickly life can shift and, at times, present unforeseen challenges that seem impossible to overcome, which can devastate our physical, emotional, and financial well-being. But often it's our setbacks—those unexpected, can't-get-up-off-the-floor moments—that create a unique opportunity for us to change course and forge a path toward new possibilities.

When I was at my lowest point in the summer of 2011, there was another woman going through a similar, though far more public and therefore far more humiliating, separation: Maria Shriver. The collapse of her marriage to former California Governor Arnold Schwarzenegger sparked a media frenzy, with details of her personal life splashed across the tabloids.

I felt this odd kinship with her, a sense that this stranger and I were traveling similar paths. She was determined to rise above the pain with grace and create a life full of purpose, empowering others through her journalism and work to fight Alzheimer's.

Ten years later, things came full circle when I had the opportunity to interview Maria. It was surreal—a God wink that still overwhelms me when I think about it. I opened our conversation with a thank-you. I wanted her to know the impact that she had on me during those very dark days when I felt so lost. I shared with her how her work inspired me to get up off that floor, wipe the tears from my eyes, and show my three sons the true meaning of resilience.

What came next was extraordinary.

Maria stopped me and expressed how much my words moved her. She shared how lonely being a writer can be. Because when you throw your work out into the world you never really know how it lands: Is it helping anyone? Is it offering a valuable perspective? You just hope your words are making an impact on someone's life. I now understand the depths of this sentiment.

Maria continued to share that during that same time she, too, was in a dark place. How often, she noted, we need to turn to other voices to learn, to be inspired, as we navigate this thing called life. Then she looked at me, smiled, and said, "I am very glad we are both up off that floor."

Amen.

Today, I am profoundly grateful for my experiences—the good, the bad, and even the truly ugly. Rebuilding my life was not easy nor was overcoming the trauma from my past. But as painful as it was, it became a gift—one that has helped me build the confidence to know, without a doubt, that I can handle whatever life throws my way. It also changed the trajectory of my journey, setting me on a path I could have never imagined.

I discovered my joy and am now living with purpose—the life I was always meant to live. I am deeply aware of how many other women find themselves facing a crisis similar to the one that ambushed me—and I know all too well how frightened and lost they can feel. Helping women create new, better lives has become my driving motivation.

The need is immense; most of us know women who have faced profound loss, upheaval, financial struggles, or trauma. Like me, the fortunate ones have used those challenges as catalysts to change their own lives—and, at times, to become agents of constructive change in the lives of others. I feel privileged to count myself among those who recognize this need and share in the intensely meaningful mission of reaching out a hand to help other women reclaim their power.

But this mission isn't for only those whose worlds have been shattered by divorce, widowhood, or financial crisis. It's not only about helping women avoid hardship; it's about empowering all women to feel more prepared for life's many twists and turns—both the lows and the highs. It's about shifting from a reactive mindset to a proactive one, especially when it comes to our financial literacy. It's about seizing opportunities, persuing dreams, and living boldly—on our own terms. This is where I want to leave you: with the understanding that life's pivotal moments—the painful ones and the joyful ones—often create exhilarating opportunities that can reinvigorate you in exciting and unexpected ways. But one of the cornerstones of this shift is financial independence—created by you, not someone else.

I hope my story helps women of all ages and circumstances see that to thrive at each turning point—whether you're rebuilding after a marriage ends, starting a new venture, redefining retirement, or launching your career after college—taking charge of your financial life (and never letting go of it) will equip you to make confident, informed decisions every step of the way.

I also hope you see the profound connection between financial autonomy and living a truly meaningful, authentic life. When fear over our financial well-being consumes us and we let it dictate our decisions, we tend to play it small, leaving no room for growth, exploration, or dreaming. We get stuck on a path that doesn't excite us and isn't aligned with who we are meant to be.

This is why the lessons in this book are so important and why I urge you to share them with every woman you know—especially your girl friends, daughters, nieces, and granddaughters. If we want better for ourselves and for the next generation, we must empower all women in our lives to thrive emotionally and financially. We also need to speak openly about our own experiences—and the stories of others—highlighting both our successes and mistakes while stressing the importance of being proactive in equipping ourselves with the tools we need to take ownership of our finances. Only then will we feel fully prepared and confident to fly—no matter what life throws our way.

Acknowledgments

If you can dream it, you can achieve it—but not without a team.

Behind every bold dream is a community of people who offer you support through your self-doubt, imposter syndrome, and the moments when quitting feels easier than pressing on.

When my life blew up over a decade ago, I had no idea where to go from there. But I knew one thing: I wanted my story to serve as both a warning and a source of inspiration for other women—no matter their age, background, or circumstance. So, I set a wild, audacious goal: I decided to write a book.

Was it a crazy idea? Absolutely. I had no writing experience and no road map. But I was determined.

I spent the next 13 years learning, growing, and working toward that dream—lifted up and guided by incredible individuals who ultimately became part of my journey, knowingly or unknowingly, encouraging me to embrace change, gain perspective, and keep moving forward. I'm so honored to now have the opportunity to share those hard-earned lessons with others.

To these people, I owe everything.

Dillon, Cole, and Drew—there are no words to express the depth of my love and gratitude to each of you. You not only kept me going during some of my darkest days, but you've also been my biggest cheerleaders from the moment I told you I wanted to write this book. Thank you for being open to me sharing the raw, vulnerable parts of our lives so that, together, we could pay it forward and help others.

Mom, you will never truly know just how deeply I love and admire you. You are more than my mother—you are my best friend. We've been through so much together. You taught me resilience, grit, and the importance of family. Thank you for allowing me to share your story, too. Our life, all those decades ago, wasn't easy. Many would have hidden from it, but you've been determined to help me help others through it—and in doing so, you've helped give it all purpose.

Matt Rauber, thank you for teaching me the true meaning of unconditional love—and the importance of wanting someone, not needing them. You stood by me through the highs and the lows, always encouraging me, holding me up, and supporting me at every turn. Just as importantly, you gave me the space to heal, to grow, and to become a better version of myself—including the mom I needed to be for my three sons. I will always be grateful for everything you did for me.

Leslie Bennetts, bestselling author, award-winning journalist, and fellow advocate for the economic empowerment of women—thank you for your unwavering support, love, and wisdom. You are so much more than a friend; you are family. I never could have written this book without you. You've always pushed me to think bigger, speak louder, and stay grounded in the importance of this work we both care so deeply about. Over the years, the impact of our friendship and professional collaboration has only reinforced what I've always believed: Everything in life truly happens for a reason—including meeting you all those years ago.

Amy Wagner, bestie, we've sure been through a lot together. At some of my lowest points, you stood by me—sitting with me in tree swings, listening without judgment, wiping my tears, and cheering me on through every turning point as I began to rebuild my life. I'll never forget your quiet strength and your constant presence.

Now, almost 15 years later, here we are—older, wiser, and still side by side, navigating this wild and beautiful life. And neither of us is playing it small anymore. I love you.

Sara McCord, you are the best damn editor! All those years ago, through every word you edited, you unknowingly became my writing coach—teaching me about structure, how to be efficient with my words, and, most importantly, the power of storytelling. It's been amazing to watch you blossom into your own success. Please know how grateful I am for your time, your talents, and your endless patience.

Austin Linthicum, you've been there from the very beginning. Thank you for your incredible design talent as I rebuilt my career and launched my businesses. You are beyond gifted, and I'm so grateful for all your help, creativity, and unwavering belief in me and my mission over the years. It's been amazing to watch you soar and build your own remarkable career—and I can't wait to see where your brilliance takes you next.

Kelly Topfer, thank you for your willingness to volunteer your time, energy, and honest feedback, which helped shape this book. I'm so grateful for your support, insight, and friendship.

To my amazing agent, Alice Martell, thank you for taking a leap of faith on me. Your guidance, belief in this story, and commitment to the process gave me the confidence to keep going, even when the road felt long.

Matt Holt, thank you for taking a chance on this first-time author. Your trust and encouragement helped bring this book to life—and for that, I am forever grateful.

Katie Dickman, you are a ROCK STAR—constantly pushing me to make this book and its insights as impactful as they can be. Thank you to you and your amazing colleagues at Matt Holt and BenBella Books. You all are nothing short of the dream team!

And lastly, Michael Page, I'm so grateful for your unwavering support, encouragement, and the hours you spent reading, rereading, and fact-checking my technical insights (and my math!). Please know how much I love and appreciate you. What a fun—and at times wild—ride it's been. Together, we've navigated the fast and the furious, including a few of life's unexpected twists and turns. Through it all, we've found laughter, love, and adventure—simply by embracing the power of saying *"Why not?"* and choosing to live fully in the moment.

Thanks to each of you (and more!) for helping make this dream a reality.

Notes

1. "2022 Marriage and Divorce Report," CDC/National Center for Health Statistics, March 13, 2024, https://www.cdc.gov/nchs/fastats/marriage-divorce.htm.

2. Kathi Balasek, "Widows Are Younger than You Think," Rethinking 65, September 7, 2022, https://rethinking65.com/widows-are-younger-than-you-think/.

3. Renee Stepler, "Led by Baby Boomers, Divorce Rates Climb for America's 50+ Population," Pew Research, March 9, 2017, https://www.pewresearch.org/short-reads/2017/03/09/led-by-baby-boomers-divorce-rates-climb-for-americas-50-population.

4. "Own Your Worth: How Women Can Break the Cycle of Abdication and Take Control of Their Wealth," UBS, 2018, https://www.ubs.com/global/de/media/display-page-ndp/en-20180514-ubs-reveals-top-reason.html#:~:text=April%2013%2C%20New%20York%2C%20NY,burden%20to%20their%20children1.

5. "Retirement Security: Women Still Face Challenges," U.S. Government Accountability Office, July 2012, https://www.gao.gov/assets/gao-12-699-highlights.pdf.

6. Timothy Grall, "Custodial Mothers and Fathers and Their Child Support," U.S. Census Bureau, May 2020, https://www.census.gov/content/dam/Census/library/publications/2020/demo/p60-269.pdf.

7. "Survey of Income and Program Participation," U.S. Census Bureau, 2018, https://www.census.gov/programs-surveys/sipp.html.

8. Grace Enda and William Gale, "How Does Gender Equality Affect Women in Retirement?" July 2020, https://www.brookings.edu /articles/how-does-gender-equality-affect-women-in-retirement/.

9. Jocelyn Frye, "Legislative Subcommittee Hearing on Universal Paid Leave and Guaranteed Access to Child Care," Testimony Before the U.S. House Committee on Ways and Means Subcommittee on Worker and Family Support, May 27, 2021.

10. "Own Your Worth: How Women Can Break the Cycle of Abdication and Take Control of Their Wealth," UBS, 2018, https://www .ubs.com/global/de/media/display-page-ndp/en-20180514-ubs-reveals -top-reason.html#:~:text=April%2013%2C%20New%20York%2C %20NY,burden%20to%20their%20children1.

11. "Who's the Better Investor—Men or Women?" Fidelity Investments study, 2017, quoted in "Investing (Beyond Your Retirement Plan)," Fidelity Investments pamphlet, 2020, https://www.fidelity.com /bin-public/060_www_fidelity_com/documents/about-fidelity/wtm -investing-beyond-retirement-reference-guide.pdf.

12. Elaine Silverstrini, "50 Years Ago, Women Won Equal Access to Credit," *Kiplinger*, October 1, 2024, https://www.kiplinger.com/personal -finance/credit-debt/years-ago-women-won-equal-access-to-credit #:~:text=Not%20that%20long%20ago%2C%20banks,helped %20women%20build%20financial%20independence.&text=As %20recently%20as%201974%2C%20banks,calculating%20their %20credit%20card%20limits.%E2%80%9D.

13. "Timeline of Legal History of Women in the United States," National Women's History Alliance, https://nationalwomenshistoryalliance.org /resources/womens-rights-movement/detailed-timeline/#:~:text=1981 %20Kirchberg%20v.,owned%20jointly%20with%20his%20wife.

14. Judith Graham, "'True Cost of Aging' Index Shows Many U.S. Seniors Can't Afford Basic Necessities," July 27, 2022, https://www.cbsnews .com/news/retirement-many-seniors-cant-afford-basic-necessities/.

15. "Everybody Dies, but Not Everybody Lives," Prince Ea, April 20, 2016, YouTube video, 5:40, https://youtu.be/ja-n5qUNRi8.

16. "How America Banks: Household Use of Banking and Financial Services," Federal Deposit Insurance Corporation (FDIC), October 25, 2022, https://www.fdic.gov/household-survey/how-america-banks-household-use-of-banking-and-financial-services.

17. "40% of U.S. Adults in Live-In Relationships Have Committed Financial Infidelity," Bankrate, January 27, 2025, https://www.bankrate.com/f/102997/x/a6625b1769/financial-infidelity-survey-press-release-2025.pdf.

18. "Depreciation Infographic: How Fast Does My New Car Lose Value?," Edmunds, September 24, 2010, https://www.edmunds.com/car-buying/how-fast-does-my-new-car-lose-value-infographic.html.

19. Nicole Dow, "More Than Half of Us Don't Keep a Budget or Know How Much We Spend," June 15, 2021, https://www.thepennyhoarder.com/budgeting/budgeting-statistics/

20. "Subscription Service Statistics and Costs," C+R Research, July 26, 2024, https://www.crresearch.com/blog/subscription-service-statistics-and-costs.

21. Andrew Marder, "Most Americans Have a Monthly Budget, but Many Still Overspend/2023 Consumer Budgeting Report," Nerd Wallet, May 30, 2023, https://www.nerdwallet.com/article/finance/data-2023-budgeting-report.

22. Matt Schulz, "49% of Americans Can't Afford a $1,000 Emergency, With Many Relying on Credit Cards for Unexpected Expenses," Lending Tree, December 11, 2023, https://www.lendingtree.com/debt-consolidation/emergency-savings-survey.

23. "Median Sales Price of Houses Sold for the United States," Federal Reserve Bank of St. Louis, April 23, 2025, https://fred.stlouisfed.org/series/MSPUS.

24. "BMO Real Financial Progress Index Report," BMO, March 7, 2023, https://about-us.bmo.com/bmo-survey-finds-american-women-significantly-less-confident-in-retiring-compared-to-men/.

25. Katherine Schaeffer, "U.S. Centenarian Population Is Projected to Quadruple Over the Next 30 Years," Pew Research Center, January 9, 2024, https://www.pewresearch.org/short-reads/2024/01/09/us-centenarian-population-is-projected-to-quadruple-over-the-next-30-years/.

26. Timothy Grall, "Custodial Mothers and Fathers and Their Child Support," U.S. Census Bureau, May 2020, https://www.census.gov/content/dam/Census/library/publications/2020/demo/p60-269.pdf.

27. Andrew Marder, "Most Americans Have a Monthly Budget, but Many Still Overspend," NerdWallet, May 30, 2023, https://www.nerdwallet.com/article/finance/data-2023-budgeting-report.

28. Katie Colt, "Resolving Medical Billing Errors Can Save You Money," Chicago Health, December 8, 2021, https://chicagohealthonline.com/resolving-medical-billing-errors/.

29. John Buzzard and Tracy (Kitten) Goldburg, "2021 Identity Fraud Study: Shifting Angles," Javelin, March 23, 2021, https://javelinstrategy.com/research/2021-identity-fraud-study-shifting-angles.

30. "Identity Protection," University of Northern Iowa, https://admissions.uni.edu/financial-aid/financial-literacy/preventing-fraud.

31. Mark Fairlie, "8 Reasons Why the Cash-Only Model Doesn't Work for Small Businesses," Business.com, https://www.business.com/articles/8-reasons-cash-model-doesnt-work-small-businesses/.

32. "Bankcard Balances Surge Past $1 Trillion as All Risk Tiers Drive Up Their Credit Card Balances," Transunion, February 15, 2024, https://www.transunion.com/blog/q4-2023-credit-industry-insights-report?atvy=%7B%22264995%22%3A%22Experience+A%22%7D.

33. "Coupon Statistics," Capital One Shopping Research, January 2, 2025, https://capitaloneshopping.com/research/coupon-statistics.

34. Bill de Blasio and Julie Menin, "From Cradle to Cane: The Cost of Being a Female Consumer: A Study of Gender Pricing in New York City," NYC Department of Consumer and Worker Protection, December 2015, https://www.nyc.gov/assets/dca/downloads/pdf/partners/Study-of-Gender-Pricing-in-NYC.pdf.

35. Charles Weijer, "A Death in the Family: Reflections on the Terri Schiavo Case," *Canadian Medical Association Journal* 172, no. 9 (2005): 1197–1198, doi: 10.1503/cmaj.050348.

36. "Mortality in the United States, 2023," CDC, December 2024, https://www.cdc.gov/nchs/products/databriefs/db521.htm#print.

37. Karen Feldscher, "Five Healthy Habits to Live By," *The Harvard Gazette*, April 30, 2018, https://news.harvard.edu/gazette/story/2018/04/5-healthy-habits-may-increase-life-expectancy-by-decade-or-more/.

38. Katherine Schaeffer, "U.S. Centenarian Population Is Projected to Quadruple Over the Next 30 Years," Pew Research Center, January 9, 2024, https://www.pewresearch.org/short-reads/2024/01/09/us-centenarian-population-is-projected-to-quadruple-over-the-next-30-years/.

39. Susan Brown and I-Fen Lin, "The Graying of Divorce: A Half Century of Change," *The Journals of Gerontology: Series B* 77, no. 9 (September 2022): 1710-1720. https://doi.org/10.1093/geronb/gbac057.

40. Janice Compton and Robert A. Pollak, "The Life Expectancy of Older Couples and Surviving Spouses," *PLoS One* 14, no. 5 (2021): e0250564, doi: 10.1371/journal.pone.0250564.

41. Phillip N. Cohen, "Family Diversity Is the New Normal for America's Children," Council on Contemporary Families, September 4, 2014, https://sites.utexas.edu/contemporaryfamilies/2014/09/04/the-new-normal/.

42. "2024 Couples and Money Study," Fidelity, 2024, https://preview.thenewsmarket.com/Previews/FINP/DocumentAssets/660835_v4.pdf.

43. Heather Reinblatt, "Financial Infidelity Report 2023: Why People Hide Purchases from Partners," Circuit, October, 6, 2023, https://getcircuit.com/teams/blog/financial-infidelity-report.

About the Author

Photo by Tisha Shuffield

Steph Wagner is a nationally recognized thought leader in women's wealth and financial empowerment. Her passion for this work is deeply personal. Her own journey—from private equity executive to stay-at-home mom to single mother facing financial uncertainty—fuels her mission to help women take control of their wealth and build lives they love.

She currently serves as National Director of Women & Wealth at Northern Trust, where she leads the firm's advisory practice for women and its *Elevating Women* platform—a national program focused on building financial confidence and helping women use their wealth to create meaningful impact in their families, businesses, and communities.

Prior to joining Northern Trust, Steph spent years advising high-net-worth women navigating major life transitions like divorce and widowhood. She also built a national consulting practice for wealth management firms seeking to better serve female clients, and founded *WomenWealthyWise*, a platform dedicated to advancing financial literacy and empowerment for women. Earlier in her career, she was vice president at Gemini Investors, a Boston-based private equity firm.

A frequent media contributor, Steph's insights have been featured in *The Wall Street Journal*, *The New York Times*, *Entrepreneur*, *Barron's*, *Bloomberg*, MatketWatch, Yahoo Finance, *Kiplinger*, and more.

She lives just outside of Austin, Texas, and is the proud mom of three grown sons. When she's not working or writing, you'll likely find her cycling, hiking, on her yoga mat, or chasing after her beloved dogs.

KEEP MOVING TOWARD FINANCIAL INDEPENDENCE

To access the Fly! workbook, as well as additional resources, check out my website

StephLWagner.com

Follow me

@steph_l_wagner   Steph L Wagner